TEST 1

TEPS

Test of English Proficiency
developed by
Seoul National University

NEW TEPS 시험 구성

영역	문제 유형	문항수	제한 시간	점수 범위
청해 Listening Comprehension	Part I: 한 문장을 듣고 이어질 대화로 가장 적절한 답 고르기 (문장 1회 청취 후 선택지 1회 청취)	10	40분	0~240점
	Part II: 짧은 대화를 듣고 이어질 대화로 가장 적절한 답 고르기 (대화 1회 청취 후 선택지 1회 청취)	10		
	Part III: 긴 대화를 듣고 질문에 가장 적절한 답 고르기 (대화 및 질문 1회 청취 후 선택지 1회 청취)	10		
	Part IV: 담화를 듣고 질문에 가장 적절한 답 고르기(1지문 1문항) (담화 및 질문 2회 청취 후 선택지 1회 청취)	6		
	신유형 Part V: 담화를 듣고 질문에 가장 적절한 답 고르기(1지문 2문항) (담화 및 질문 2회 청취 후 선택지 1회 청취)	4		
어휘 Vocabulary	Part I: 대화문의 빈칸에 가장 적절한 어휘 고르기	10	통합 25분	0~60점
	Part II: 단문의 빈칸에 가장 적절한 어휘 고르기	20		
문법 Grammar	Part I: 대화문의 빈칸에 가장 적절한 답 고르기	10		0~60점
	Part II: 단문의 빈칸에 가장 적절한 답 고르기	15		
	Part III: 대화 및 문단에서 문법상 틀리거나 어색한 부분 고르기	5		
독해 Reading Comprehension	Part I: 지문을 읽고 빈칸에 가장 적절한 답 고르기	10	40분	0~240점
	Part II: 지문을 읽고 문맥상 어색한 내용 고르기	2		
	Part III: 지문을 읽고 질문에 가장 적절한 답 고르기(1지문 1문항)	13		
	신유형 Part IV: 지문을 읽고 질문에 가장 적절한 답 고르기(1지문 2문항)	10		
총계	14개 Parts	135문항	105분	0~600점

TEPS

LISTENING COMPREHENSION

DIRECTIONS

1. In the Listening Comprehension section, all content will be presented orally rather than in written form.
2. This section contains five parts. For each part, you will receive separate instructions. Listen to the instructions carefully, and choose the best answer from the options for each item.

MP3 바로 듣기
해석·해설 확인
받아쓰기 테스트

Part I Questions 1~10

You will now hear ten individual spoken questions or statements, each followed by four spoken responses. Choose the most appropriate response for each item.

Part II Questions 11~20

You will now hear ten short conversation fragments, each followed by four spoken responses. Choose the most appropriate response to complete each conversation.

Part III   Questions 21~30

You will now hear ten complete conversations. For each conversation, you will be asked to answer a question. Before each conversation, you will hear a short description of the situation. After listening to the description and conversation once, you will hear a question and four options. Based on the given information, choose the option that best answers the question.

Part IV Questions 31~36

You will now hear six short talks. After each talk, you will be asked to answer a question. Each talk and its corresponding question will be read twice. Then you will hear four options which will be read only once. Based on the given information, choose the option that best answers the question.

Part V Questions 37~40

You will now hear two longer talks. After each talk, you will be asked to answer two questions. Each talk and its corresponding questions will be read twice. However, the four options for each question will be read only once. Based on the given information, choose the option that best answers each question.

TEPS

VOCABULARY & GRAMMAR

DIRECTIONS

These two sections test your vocabulary and grammar knowledge. You will have 25 minutes to complete a total of 60 questions: 30 from the Vocabulary section and 30 from the Grammar section. Be sure to follow the directions given by the proctor.

Part I Questions 1~10

Choose the option that best completes each dialogue.

1. A: What time are we meeting for dinner tonight?
   B: I haven't _____.
   (a) made
   (b) fixed
   (c) decided
   (d) realized

2. A: Trenton simply _____ calm, doesn't he?
   B: Yeah, he's so relaxing to be around.
   (a) steels
   (b) injects
   (c) exudes
   (d) protrudes

3. A: What are you in the mood for right now?
   B: It's so hot. A big ice cream cone sure would _____.
   (a) hit the spot
   (b) toe the line
   (c) miss the mark
   (d) weather the storm

4. A: You don't see many 7-11's in the US anymore.
   B: Right, but they're _____ in Asia.
   (a) ubiquitous
   (b) transitory
   (c) systemic
   (d) omniscient

5. A: What are you doing _____ through the kitchen cabinets?
   B: I can't seem to find the pressure cooker.
   (a) condescending
   (b) rummaging
   (c) showcasing
   (d) simmering

6. A: I heard your company broadened its sick leave policy.
   B: Yeah, and they applied it _____ to the beginning of last year.
   (a) markedly
   (b) retroactively
   (c) complacently
   (d) simultaneously

7. A: I'm so nervous about the job interview.
   B: Just take a _____ breath. You'll do fine.
   (a) sour
   (b) cool
   (c) deep
   (d) mute

8. A: Do you feel a(n) _____? Where's that coming from?
   B: I must have left the bedroom window open.
   (a) vent
   (b) draft
   (c) fan
   (d) air

9. A: Lincolnville is experiencing a homelessness crisis.
   B: I know. So many _____ people are living on the streets.
   (a) commensurate
   (b) resultant
   (c) destitute
   (d) egregious

10. A: There are lots of rumors of company layoffs next month.
    B: Yeah, I've heard about them _____ myself.
    (a) through the grapevine
    (b) once in a blue moon
    (c) with a grain of salt
    (d) off the bat

Part II Questions 11~30

Choose the option that best completes each sentence.

11. Mustafa Kemal Atatürk, founder of modern-day Turkey, is still _____ as a national hero.

    (a) revered
    (b) covered
    (c) abstained
    (d) formatted

12. Residents are so accustomed to tornado alerts that many do not _____ the warnings.

    (a) heed
    (b) elicit
    (c) impose
    (d) stipulate

13. A proposed national park would preserve a significant portion of the lesser prairie chicken's _____.

    (a) compound
    (b) residence
    (c) dwelling
    (d) habitat

14. When inflation _____ wage increases, more and more citizens begin to slide into poverty.

    (a) adores
    (b) outpaces
    (c) touts
    (d) shocks

15. Financial regulators will be implementing new _____ measures to lessen the risk of a collapse.

    (a) precautionary
    (b) bicentennial
    (c) laudatory
    (d) invasive

16. William the Conqueror led his troops to _____ in the Norman invasion of Britain in 1066.

    (a) vanity
    (b) serenity
    (c) civility
    (d) victory

17. _____ of fresh Maine lobster arrive at Terry's Seafood Shack at least twice weekly.

    (a) Dollops
    (b) Cascades
    (c) Shipments
    (d) Promotions

18. Once its primary natural predator was removed, the bullfrog was able to _____ and spread unchecked.

    (a) propagate
    (b) renovate
    (c) mitigate
    (d) dilate

19. A large percentage of Iranians would prefer the country's ruling clerics to adopt a more _____ stance.

    (a) mordant
    (b) sniveling
    (c) litigious
    (d) secular

20. The film, _____ with scenes of sex and violence, earned an adult-only rating from the advisory board.

    (a) administered
    (b) combined
    (c) dubious
    (d) replete

21. Homeowners who make the switch to solar power will see a return on their _____ in roughly 12 years.

    (a) sentimentality
    (b) investment
    (c) opulence
    (d) defect

22. Rare instances of fatal throat inflammation have been _____ in clinical trials of the drug.

    (a) flaunted
    (b) observed
    (c) reasoned
    (d) neglected

23. Medieval artists depended largely on the _____ of their benefactors in order to survive.

    (a) largess
    (b) penalty
    (c) symptom
    (d) countenance

24. The new golf course features a groundbreaking _____ system that captures and reuses 90% of rainwater runoff.

    (a) membership
    (b) irrigation
    (c) leisure
    (d) germ

25. Scientists were able to _____ the mountain lion long enough to implant a tracking device behind its ear.

    (a) hinder
    (b) sedate
    (c) prolong
    (d) withstand

26. The portable typewriters of the early 1900s were, in essence, the _____ of the modern-day laptop.

    (a) innovators
    (b) instigators
    (c) forerunners
    (d) competitors

27. _____ of abuse of performance-enhancing drugs were raised even before the cyclist had received the champion's trophy.

    (a) Liaisons
    (b) Accusations
    (c) Machinations
    (d) Embodiments

28. Physicians are unable to _____ illnesses based on a patient's family medical history alone.

    (a) prescribe
    (b) diagnose
    (c) advance
    (d) operate

29. Germany's mistreatment by the international community following WWI is often _____ as a cause of Hitler's rise to power.

    (a) cited
    (b) sought
    (c) gratified
    (d) unhinged

30. Despite a handful of _____ reviews, most critics responded positively to the war hero's memoir.

    (a) amenable
    (b) prognostic
    (c) disparaging
    (d) misappropriated

You have finished the Vocabulary questions. Please continue on to the Grammar questions.

Part I Questions 1~10

Choose the option that best completes each dialogue.

1. A: Why do you use this set of gym equipment?
   B: Because it _____ a full-body workout.
   (a) provided
   (b) provides
   (c) had provided
   (d) has provided

2. A: It's a shame Catherine didn't arrive sooner.
   B: Yes, her _____ late really wrecked our plans.
   (a) had been
   (b) to be
   (c) being
   (d) was

3. A: Let's call a plumber to fix the leaky faucet.
   B: Or, _____, we could do the work ourselves.
   (a) better yet
   (b) yet better
   (c) better it's yet
   (d) it's yet better

4. A: Does Michelle know the workshop schedule?
   B: I doubt it. But luckily I _____.
   (a) do
   (b) have
   (c) do now
   (d) will have

5. A: My computer is running way too hot. It must be broken.
   B: Hmm, you're right. It _____ that.
   (a) couldn't do
   (b) might not do
   (c) shouldn't be doing
   (d) won't have been doing

6. A: This snowstorm is turning into a disaster.
   B: Yeah, _____ have already been reported.
   (a) traffic accidents several major
   (b) several major traffic accidents
   (c) major several traffic accidents
   (d) several traffic major accidents

7. A: Why did you buy another secondhand canoe?
   B: Hey, I can't _____ a good deal.
   (a) back turn on
   (b) turn back on
   (c) turn my back on
   (d) back on my turn

8. A: I can't believe you're asking for a 10% raise!
   B: Well, I _____.
   (a) entitled it I feel to
   (b) feel I'm entitled to it
   (c) am entitled to feel it
   (d) feel it I'm entitled to

9. A: The B&L merger fell through yesterday.
   B: Yes, experts say their stock could drop by _____ 50%.
   (a) a lot of
   (b) as many
   (c) more of
   (d) as much as

10. A: Any word yet from the authorities?
    B: So far they're _____ to wait.
    (a) to everyone urging
    (b) just urging everyone
    (c) everyone urging just
    (d) urging of everyone should

Part II Questions 11~25

Choose the option that best completes each sentence.

11. The suspect in question had been observed _____ of the stolen goods before he fled.

(a) dispose
(b) disposing
(c) to be disposed
(d) being disposed

12. _____ for the pilot's extensive safety training, the plane surely would have crashed and been destroyed.

(a) It being had
(b) It hadn't been
(c) Had it not been
(d) Having not been

13. Average air temperatures in Antarctica are typically around 30 degrees colder _____ the Arctic.

(a) those than
(b) than those
(c) than those of
(d) of those than

14. Just before Amy was scheduled to speak, she _____ with a severe bout of anxiety.

(a) has been striking
(b) was to strike
(c) had struck
(d) was struck

15. A majority of journalists surveyed said they found _____ objective during the lead-up to the Iraq War difficult.

(a) remains
(b) to remain
(c) remaining
(d) having remained

16. Per tradition, Moroccans _____ visitors with a glass of mint tea as soon as they arrive.

(a) greet
(b) to greet
(c) had greeted
(d) had been greeted

17. _____ the poll numbers were against him, the candidate announced that he would drop out of the race.

(a) Realizing
(b) To realize
(c) Realizes
(d) Realized

18. _____ a crime he did not commit, Earl Jones is being released after serving 25 years.

(a) Has convicted of being
(b) Convicted of having been
(c) Having been convicted of
(d) Being convicted of having

19. _____ their country is free of Soviet influence, young, well-educated Mongolians are rediscovering their religious heritage.

(a) It is
(b) Is that
(c) That now
(d) Now that

20. Medical researchers have found a relationship _____ one's exposure to secondhand smoke and one's risk of sinus disease.

(a) among
(b) through
(c) around
(d) between

21. Airlines are encouraged to develop rerouting contingency plans _____ unforeseen natural or manmade disasters.

    (a) notwithstanding
    (b) even though
    (c) on par with
    (d) in case of

22. Two top law firms are courting Allen Burt, but he appears interested in _____ of them.

    (a) either
    (b) lesser
    (c) neither
    (d) whether

23. Investors were unable to do _____ sit back helplessly and watch their holdings vanish.

    (a) the most
    (b) more of
    (c) much more than
    (d) enough more than

24. Miami, _____ by four Class 4 hurricanes within the span of a month, faces daunting repair needs.

    (a) devastated
    (b) devastating
    (c) it was devastated
    (d) being devastating

25. The accused criminal's safety _____ by local police, so he was transferred to a federal facility.

    (a) not guaranteed
    (b) cannot guarantee
    (c) did not guarantee
    (d) could not be guaranteed

Part III Questions 26~30

Read each dialogue or passage carefully and identify the option that contains a grammatical error.

26. (a) A: Students' stress is at an all-time high.
(b) B: Is that what you heard from the school counselor?
(c) A: That's right. He says he's never seen it so badly.
(d) B: It's caused by parents putting too much pressure on their kids.

27. (a) A: Hi, I'd like to return this coat. It's too small.
(b) B: Oh, I'm sorry. We didn't accept returns on sale items.
(c) A: You're kidding me. That's a ridiculous rule.
(d) B: What can I say? It's store policy.

28. (a) In the US, areas of severe hazardous contamination are designated Superfund sites. (b) As such, they benefit from federal funds set aside specifically to clean such areas. (c) Abandoned chemical factories, obsolete garbage dumps, and toxic spill sites are examples of typical Superfund sites. (d) They exist in all 50 states and several of US territories, with more being added on a regular basis.

29. (a) Geologists use the Mohs scale of hardness to rate the scratch resistance of different rocks and minerals. (b) Basically, each specimen is assigned a rating according to which softer materials it is able to scratch and which harder materials can scratch it. (c) Thus, all the rocks and minerals on Earth is laid out along a single spectrum of hardness. (d) The system was created by German mineralogist Friedrich Mohs in 1812.

30. (a) For those looking to get healthy, one useful tactic is to eat through the color spectrum each day. (b) The simple fact is that foods containing the most beneficial vitamins also possess distinct colors. (c) Ensuring your plate displays bright colors of a variety also ensures you are getting your daily dose of fruits and vegetables. (d) So the next time you sit down to eat, try tasting your food with your eyes as well as your mouth.

You have reached the end of the Vocabulary & Grammar sections. Do NOT move on to the Reading Comprehension section until instructed to do so. You are NOT allowed to turn to any other section of the test.

TEPS

Reading Comprehension

Directions

This section tests your ability to comprehend reading passages. You will have 40 minutes to complete 35 questions. Be sure to follow the directions given by the proctor.

Part I Questions 1~10

Read the passage and choose the option that best completes the passage.

1. With winter fast approaching, are you dreading paying the sky-high cost of natural gas, electric, or oil heating? We at Peterson Woodstove Solutions understand. So we are here to help you _____. With a Peterson certified woodstove, you can cut your monthly heating bill in half. Come by one of our three convenient locations today and our representatives will help you find the stove that is right for your home.

   (a) retrofit your existing gas- or oil-burning stove
   (b) escape the cycle of exorbitant heating costs
   (c) insulate your home from the chill of winter
   (d) discover the benefits of woodstove cooking

2.
   Dear Editor,

   I have serious misgivings about the "Toddler Tube" series that appears weekly in your newspaper recommending children's television shows to parents. A new study is out claiming that any exposure to television at age two will make children less engaged in school and more likely to be overweight. How can you, as an influential community institution, encourage parents to sit their toddlers in front of the TV _____?

   Deeply concerned,
   Janice

   (a) in light of these shocking statistics
   (b) with all the violence on television
   (c) and expose them to such advertising
   (d) for more than two hours a week

3. Are you a constant sufferer of buyer's remorse? If so, _____. That's according to psychologists who have tested the ability of hand washing to counteract the natural doubts people experience after they make a decision. Participants were asked to sample 10 music CDs and then choose one to take home with them. Half were immediately prompted to wash their hands after the decision, and the other half were not. Those who washed up reported more contentment with their selection than those who did not.

   (a) washing what you buy is the answer
   (b) perhaps you should wash up more often
   (c) buying hand washing products will not help
   (d) you have subconscious concerns over hygiene

4. Fault zones are sites where two or more portions of the Earth intersect one another, and they often give rise to earthquakes. However, some are like long-dormant volcanoes in that they pose no risk to human populations. An example is the Balcones Fault of central Texas. It was formed during the creation of the nearby Ouachita Mountains some 300 million years ago, and indeed the region experienced frequent earthquakes up until 15 million years ago. Nowadays the Balcones Fault is _____.

(a) no longer an active earthquake zone
(b) carefully monitored by seismologists
(c) barely visible in the central Texas area
(d) responsible for tremors throughout Texas

5. Astronomers have discovered a method for _____.
A new instrument is being used to combine readings from four of the world's most powerful telescopes, and the composite data is shedding more light on extraterrestrial star systems than any of the individual telescopes could do on their own. The most significant finding thus far has been the presence of discs of dust and other matter in orbit around nearby stars. These systems resemble our early Solar System, and perhaps they too will eventually form Earth-like planets.

(a) calculating the distances to faraway solar systems
(b) peering into the solar systems of our stellar neighbors
(c) detecting Earth-like planets outside of our Solar System
(d) analyzing the data collected by multiple space telescopes

6. According to early accounts from its opening weekend, Max Whitman's documentary *In Deep Fog* _____. Critics and ordinary moviegoers alike are praising its controversial depiction of elder abuse in Alzheimer's wards around the country. In addition to bringing to light the prevalence and severity of this social crisis, Whitman has done so in an artful, dignified, and professional manner. Many doubted whether early publicity and claims surrounding the film would be answered with real substance, but it appears those doubts were unfounded.

    (a) contains footage not suitable for everyone
    (b) has lived up to the pre-release hype
    (c) will lead to changes in elder care
    (d) will not break box-office records

7. England's canal system dates back to Roman times, when the waterways were developed to aid in crop irrigation. They continued to be used in this fashion throughout the Middle Ages, in addition providing cargo routes for intra-island commerce. However, it was during the onset of the Industrial Revolution in the late 1700s that _____. With road conditions unreliable, canals provided direct links between inland factories and coastal ports, propelling England to the forefront of a new era.

    (a) local farmers began using the canals
    (b) the history of the canals was understood
    (c) canals were opened for public use instead
    (d) the canals became the lifelines of the nation

8. During the US Civil War, there was no battle so decisive as that of Gettysburg, and the outcome of this most bloody engagement hinged on the fighting at a hill called Little Round Top. Holding the line for the Union troops, hunkered down on the hill's south slope and commanded by Colonel Joshua Chamberlain, were the men of the 20th Maine. With minimal manpower and ammunition, they withstood charge after charge of Confederate Alabamians seeking to dislodge them from the strategic high ground of Little Round Top. Their tenacity prevented the attackers from achieving this objective and _____.

    (a) nearly destroyed Little Round Top
    (b) spelled defeat for the Confederates
    (c) took the Union troops by surprise
    (d) adversely affected troop morale

9. With Greece set to default on the majority of its loans to international investors, the rest of Europe has at last agreed to a nearly trillion-dollar rescue package to shore up faith in the euro. This was despite strong voter discontent in countries like Germany, where citizens are reluctant to initiate a trend of bailouts to weaker euro-zone members. Investors, _____, have responded positively. Markets around the globe have gained value since the announcement.

   (a) likewise
   (b) as a result
   (c) in other words
   (d) on the other hand

10.
   ### Science Report

   We are taught the importance of a good night's sleep from a young age, but now scientists have the proof. A new study in Italy has shown that individuals who average fewer than six hours of sleep per night are over 10 percent more likely to die prematurely. _____, the results also raised concerns about habitual "long sleeping" (9 or more hours a night), and scientists warn that long sleep is often a symptom of serious illnesses that in turn carry an increased risk of death. Never have the health benefits of a solid 6-8 hours sleep been so solidly documented.

   (a) Therefore
   (b) At the same time
   (c) Notwithstanding
   (d) Without a doubt

Part II Questions 11~12

Read the passage and identify the option that does NOT belong.

11. NASA has successfully launched the Space Shuttle Atlantis on what is likely to be its final mission. (a) The space vehicle began its service in October of 1985, when it assisted in the launch of two military satellites. (b) Its charge is to deliver a Russian-built module to the International Space Station, where it will be installed. (c) Upon return, Atlantis is scheduled for decommissioning, with NASA's two remaining shuttles awaiting a similar fate later this year. (d) However, officials have announced that Atlantis could be used in an emergency rescue mission in the near future should the need arise.

12. Though there are many types of blood disorders, anemia is the most common. (a) It is marked by a decreased abundance of red blood cells and/or hemoglobin in the blood. (b) Since these structures are responsible for delivering oxygen to the body's organs, their absence can have serious health repercussions. (c) Treatment options for anemia range from simple iron supplements to periodic blood transfusions. (d) In the severest of cases, a patient may experience a fatal condition such as heart failure.

Part III Questions 13~25

Read the passage, question, and options. Then, based on the given information, choose the option that best answers each question.

13. More than three million years ago, the ancestors of modern humans were still living in trees. However, research suggests that these early hominids could also walk on two feet with a human-like stride. The research is based on fossil footprints preserved in volcanic ash deposited 3.6 million years ago in what is modern-day Tanzania. The most likely explanation for the prints is that they were made by a bipedal species. Indeed, skeletons of this species have a number of features in the hips, legs, and back that indicate that they would have walked on two legs.

Q: What is the main idea of the passage?
(a) Human ancestors once lived in trees in the region of Tanzania.
(b) Tree-dwelling ancestors of humans lived 3.6 million years ago.
(c) Research shows that bipedal fossil prints were made by humans.
(d) Evidence indicates tree-dwelling human ancestors were bipedal.

14.
Palm Isle

Escape to Palm Isle and leave your troubles far behind. Whether it is sun tanning, diving, hiking, swimming, or sailing, Palm Isle has something for you. Stroll the spectacular blond beaches and tropical palm groves or swim in pristine turquoise waters. Ride in a glass-bottom boat and then spend the afternoon playing a round of golf on our world-class course. At the end of the day, walk up the Wilderness Trail to Vista Point for the best sunset views on the island.

Q: What is mainly being advertised?
(a) A glass-bottom boat ride in one of Palm Isle's bays
(b) Hiking opportunities on a forested tropical island
(c) An island destination and its various activities
(d) Tour options at a large, family-oriented resort

15. When it was completed in 1877, Leo Tolstoy's novel *Anna Karenina* was spurned by Russian literary critics, who considered the text trivial, as just another inconsequential romance. Other writers, however, like Dostoevsky and Nabokov, recognized the novel's merits and heralded *Anna Karenina* as a literary masterpiece. They appreciated the subtle motifs, moving language, and powerful themes that today accord *Anna Karenina* high esteem. Indeed, some contemporary critics regard the work as one of the best novels ever written.

Q: What is the passage mainly about?
(a) Dominant historical themes in *Anna Karenina*
(b) The manner in which Tolstoy wrote *Anna Karenina*
(c) The reception of *Anna Karenina* and its current status
(d) Dostoevsky and Nabokov's opinions of *Anna Karenina*

16. In the early twentieth century, Antarctica attracted scores of ambitious pioneers who hoped their polar explorations would earn them a place in history. One such individual was Roald Amundsen, a Norwegian expedition leader whose name is legendary among Antarctic explorers. He led the first successful mission to the South Pole, arriving on December 14, 1911. This historic achievement was Amundsen's by only a small margin, for the English explorer Robert Scott arrived at the South Pole just thirty-five days later.

Q: What is the main topic of the article?
(a) Antarctic attractions for explorers
(b) Amundsen's Victory Narrowly Won
(c) A Forgotten Figure in Antarctic History
(d) Norwegian Explorers First to Antarctica

17. The name Charles Darwin is a familiar one, as most of us have at one time or another studied the renowned English naturalist who came up with the theory of natural selection. However, the name also belonged to the naturalist's uncle, who lived between 1758 and 1778. This "other" Charles Darwin also had a special interest in science, which he applied to the study of medicine. He attended medical school in Edinburgh, but, tragically, died at the age of twenty before becoming a physician.

Q: Which of the following is correct about the "other" Charles Darwin?
(a) He was related to Charles Darwin as his uncle.
(b) He also studied the theory of natural selection.
(c) He studied science before turning to medicine.
(d) He was employed as a physician in Edinburgh.

18. Inspired by the long poems of his compatriot Walt Whitman, the poet Hart Crane poured his creativity into what would become his masterpiece, a book-length poem called *The Bridge*. Yet, upon its publication, the poem was declared a failure. The public regarded his writing as opaque and difficult. But among his contemporaries and the generation of poets that followed, Crane was upheld as a muse, a source of stimulation and insight. Today, Crane is affectionately regarded as "a poet's poet."

Q: Which of the following is correct according to the passage?
(a) Whitman was inspired by Crane's *The Bridge*.
(b) *The Bridge* was well received when published.
(c) The public did not initially appreciate Crane's work.
(d) Crane has largely been forgotten by contemporary poets.

19. The Sufi writer Sanai once served as a poet in the court of Bahram-shah. According to legend, while preparing to accompany Bahram-shah on a military campaign to India, Sanai overheard the Sufi teacher Lai-khur criticizing him for blindly praising the greedy and foolish Bahram-shah and following him on the senseless India campaign. Sanai was shamed by these words, but he recognized their truth. He withdrew from the court and embarked on a pilgrimage. Upon his return, he wrote *Hadiqat-ul HaqiqahI*, or *The Walled Garden of Truth*, which is still read as a classic Sufi text.

Q: Which is correct about Sanai according to the passage?
(a) He fought in India alongside Bahram-shah.
(b) He rejected being spoken to critically by Lai-khur.
(c) He refused to accept anyone's criticism.
(d) He exiled himself from the royal court.

20. It's a common misconception that a business can set prices by determining its present operating costs and formulating a price that will cover those costs plus produce a profit. This is what's known as a fixed-cost price model, and unfortunately it does not apply to real-world scenarios. The flaw lies in the fact that operating costs don't remain constant over time. As it grows, the business will take on more employees, develop higher equipment costs, etc. Therefore, charging the lowest prices possible to turn a profit under the fixed-cost model will ultimately drive the company out of business. Instead, a variable-cost price model must be employed.

Q: Which of the following is correct about fixed-cost price models?
(a) They tend to reflect real life situations.
(b) They fail to account for future cost hikes.
(c) They are one way to effect business growth.
(d) They are superior to some variable-cost models.

21.

Dear Homeowner:

On behalf of the Norton Woods community, I would like to extend to you a warm welcome to the neighborhood. As you are new to the area, I would like to call your attention to a violation of the Norton Woods Homeowners Association agreement of which you might not be aware. In accordance with these rules, which were put in place to enhance your community, the trash bins in your driveway must be removed and stowed where they will not be visible from the street. Thank you for your compliance.

Sincerely,
Gillian Dorsey
Director

Q: Which of the following is correct according to the letter?
(a) Violations were committed by the homeowners association.
(b) Homeowners must leave trash bins out for collection.
(c) Norton Woods community rules recently changed.
(d) Trash bins are not to be kept in driveways.

22. The Colombian novelist Gabriel García Márquez is one of the most revered and beloved writers within the pantheon of Latin American authors. Although he worked as a journalist, wrote numerous short stories and nonfiction works, García Márquez is best known for his novel *One Hundred Years of Solitude*. The book is a chronicle of the Buendía family in the fictional town of Macondo. Published in 1967, it was an international success and was received with much critical acclaim. In the years since its publication, it has been translated into more than 30 languages.

Q: Which of the following is correct according to the passage?
(a) Journalism made García Márquez famous.
(b) García Márquez was exclusively a fiction writer.
(c) *One Hundred Years of Solitude* is a nonfiction work.
(d) García Márquez's work is available in many languages.

23.

> To the Editor:
>
> In my opinion, your article on Houston's proposed streetcars in last Thursday's issue of the *Times* utterly missed the mark. Rather than investigating the relative merits of buses and streetcars, as author Keith Mahoney did, you ought to be asking why the municipal government is investing so many tax dollars into implementing a system that is so hopelessly inefficient. Streetcars may run on electricity, but since they require rails they are much more costly to install and maintain than other mass transit systems, like trolley buses.
>
> Rosaline Bouchard

Q: What can be inferred about the writer from the letter?
(a) She opposes the pending streetcar system.
(b) She supports the investigation done by Mahoney.
(c) She does not feel mass transit is worth the expense.
(d) She is a member of the Houston municipal government.

24. Known for his singular style and his eye for color, the French artist Paul Cézanne renounced the quiet conventions of Impressionism—which predominated during the 19th century—and forged a post-Impressionist aesthetic that was related to its predecessor. His painting was brighter, more geometric, and more expressive. His most revolutionary works have bold, un-lifelike color and multiple views of a single subject, a concept central to Cubism. Traversing the artistic territory between Impressionism and Cubism through his experimental work, Cézanne inspired some of the great modernist artists of the 20th century, like Picasso and Matisse.

Q: What can be inferred about Cézanne according to the passage?
(a) He is best known for launching Impressionism.
(b) Picasso was inspired by him more than anyone else.
(c) Picasso and Matisse worked with him to develop Cubism.
(d) He represents a transition from Impressionism to modernism.

25.

> **Notice**
>
> To all residents,
>
> Do not use one of the eastern elevators which is in need of replacement of defective parts. We'll repair it as soon as possible. We apologize for any inconvenience this may cause you.
>
> After that, continue using the existing elevators for a while. Three months later, one elevator in the west and east will be replaced by the latest model as you requested.
>
> Thank you for your proposals to improve this building.
>
> **Maintenance department, Tribune Tower**

Q: What can be inferred about the Tribune Tower?
(a) Some residents should leave the Tower within three months.
(b) It will be fully remodeled with new interior.
(c) An occupant's proposal is accepted.
(d) It is not yet ready for occupancy.

Part IV Questions 26~35

Read the passage, questions, and options. Then, based on the given information, choose the option that best answers each question.

Questions 26-27

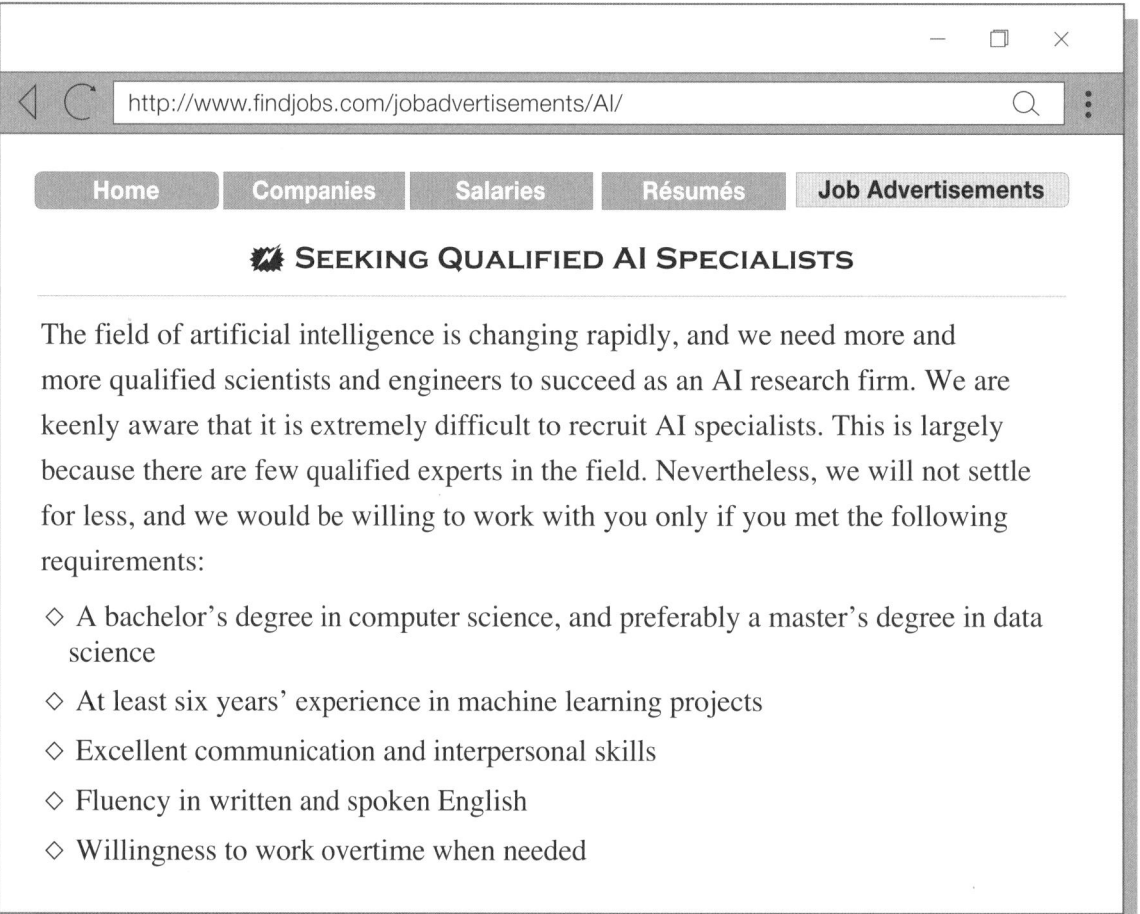

26. Q: Which of the following is correct according to the passage?

   (a) At present, there are so many AI specialists that the company cannot hire all of them.
   (b) The company does not recruit college graduates.
   (c) The company has no intention of lowering its hiring standards.
   (d) A renowned scientist founded the company.

27. Q: What can be inferred from the passage?

   (a) The company remains pessimistic about the growth of the field of artificial intelligence.
   (b) Successful candidates will work only with native speakers of English.
   (c) Machine learning was developed simultaneously with artificial intelligence.
   (d) Communication is likely to be an important part of the advertised job.

Questions 28-29

His Childhood Helped to Shape His Future

Most people think of Elon Musk as an extraordinary businessman. This is mainly because he founded and co-founded so many companies, such as SpaceX and Tesla Motors. Nevertheless, Musk is basically an engineer. He once said, "I'm an engineer, so what I do is engineering." As an engineer, he has been dedicating himself to improving space exploration and clean-energy technologies.

His childhood may have prepared him for his illustrious career as an engineer. Although his childhood was not a happy one, reading books brought him great joy. He read lots of books throughout his childhood. As a result, he became aware of the power of knowledge. At the same time, he realized that computing had great potential. When he turned ten, he became interested in computing. He mastered computer programming when he was twelve. He even invented a video game based on BASIC programming. Musk's talent was to shine through in technology.

28. Q: What is the passage mainly about?

    (a) What qualities have allowed Musk to thrive as a successful businessman
    (b) How Musk's talent in technology was formed and shone through
    (c) Why deprived childhoods often lead to successful careers in technology
    (d) Why avid readers such as Musk tend to overcome difficulties in life

29. Q: What can be inferred about Musk from the passage?

    (a) He regards himself as an exceptional businessman.
    (b) He is written off as a fraud by eminent scientists and engineers.
    (c) He is convinced that space exploration technology will make him one of the wealthiest people in the world.
    (d) His childhood was devoted to gaining knowledge and developing computing skills.

Questions 30-31

Flowers and Fragrances for Every Woman

Every woman loves flowers and fragrances. But how can you find the perfect flowers and fragrances for your special woman? *Flowers and Fragrances for Every Woman* is here to help you do that! You don't even have to ask around to find out what her favorite flowers and fragrances are.

Here at *Flowers and Fragrances for Every Woman*, you'll be surprised by the amazing variety of flowers and fragrances you can choose from. Our collection of flowers and fragrances is so vast that you can easily find the perfect gift for your special woman. Plus, our same-day delivery services make sure that she will receive your perfect gift any day you want. For further information, visit our website at www.flowers&fragrances.com.

30. Q: Which of the following is correct about the store, according to the passage?

(a) It specializes in catering to high-end customers.
(b) It helps women to choose the perfect fragrances for their spouses.
(c) Its customer can get his order delivered on the same day as he orders it.
(d) Its Web site is still under construction.

31. Q: What can be inferred from the advertisement?

(a) Women's penchant for flowers and fragrances is not well-known.
(b) The store has conducted a survey of women about their preferences for flowers and fragrances.
(c) The store delivers its goods all over the world.
(d) Those men who are pressed for time are likely to find the store's service helpful.

Questions 32-33

POLITICS > LOCAL   *The Richville Times*

City Council's Decision Raises Ire of Environmental Groups

The City Council of Richville has recently announced that it will approve the full deregulation of the tourism industry. The City of Richville has already deregulated 45% of the industry, which has helped to attract more and more tourists from foreign countries. When the tourism industry is completely deregulated, the City of Richville is likely to boost its economy significantly.

However, environmental groups have severely criticized the City Council for sacrificing the city's natural environment for economic gain. They have repeatedly pointed out that more tourists mean more pollution. According to them, with the tourism industry booming, the city has been suffering environmental degradation, including air pollution. In an effort to prevent further degradation, the environmental groups are urging the City Council to reconsider its decision.

32. Q: What percentage of the tourism industry is currently NOT deregulated?

(a) 40%
(b) 45%
(c) 50%
(d) 55%

33. Q: Why are the environmental groups against the City Council's decision?

(a) Because they have xenophobic attitudes toward foreign tourists.
(b) Because they are not convinced that the tourism industry will contribute to the economic prosperity of Richville.
(c) Because they are particularly concerned about the effects of global warming on Richville.
(d) Because they are concerned that the booming tourism will adversely affect the natural environment of Richville.

Questions 34-35

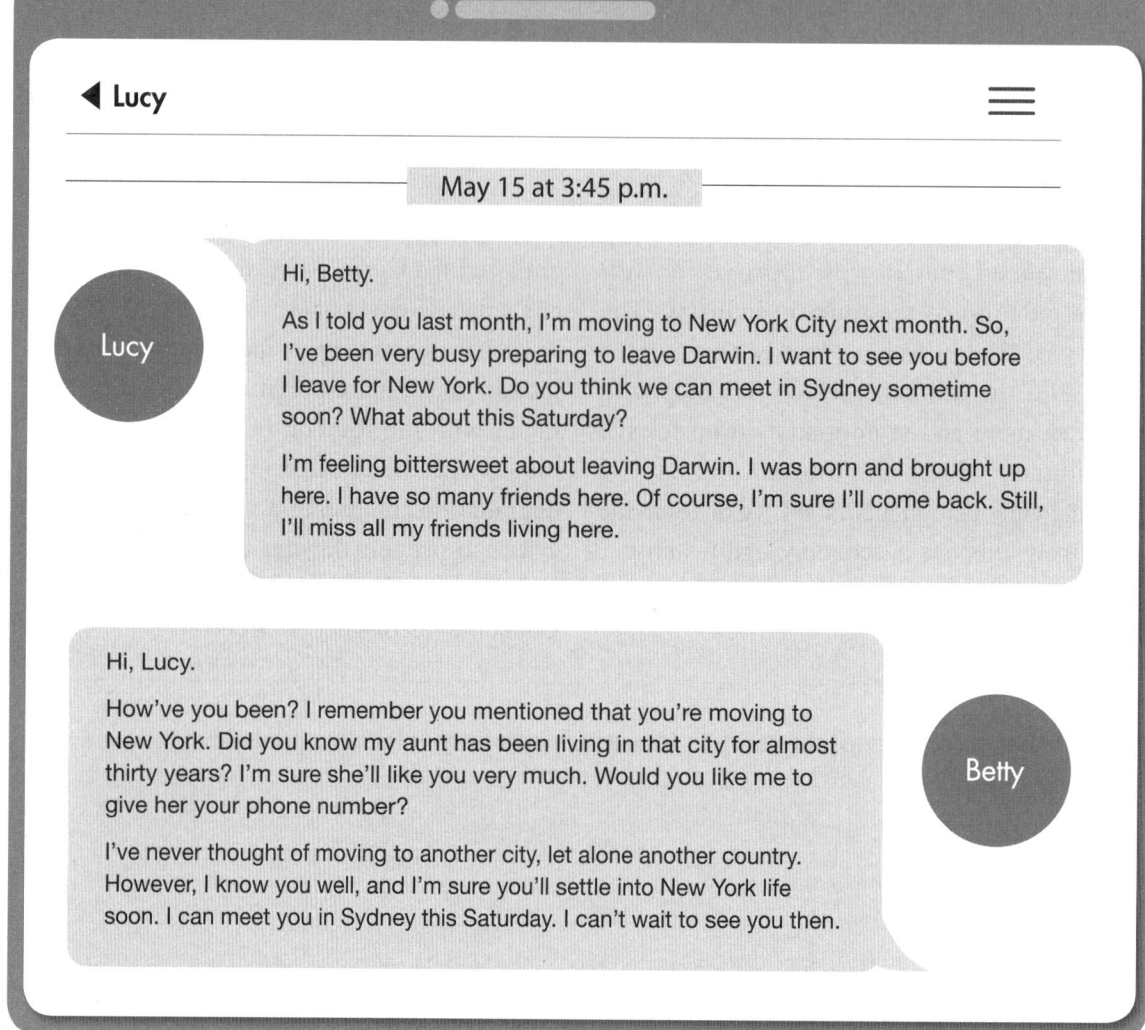

34. Q: Why did Lucy send the message?

(a) She wants to meet Betty's aunt in New York.
(b) She wants to raise her children in Darwin.
(c) She wants to see some friends in Sydney.
(d) She wants to bid farewell to Betty before leaving Darwin.

35. Q: What can be inferred from the chat messages?

(a) Lucy met Betty in Darwin last month.
(b) Lucy prefers to lead a nomadic lifestyle.
(c) Betty's aunt has a rewarding job in a professional field.
(d) Betty may live permanently in her current city.

You have reached the end of the Reading Comprehension section. Please remain seated until you are dismissed by the proctor. You are NOT allowed to turn to any other section of the test.

TEPS
Test of English Proficiency developed by Seoul National University

TEPS

Test of English Proficiency
developed by
Seoul National University

응시일자 : 20   년   월   일

<부정행위 및 규정위반 처리규정>

1. 모든 부정행위 및 규정위반 적발 및 이에 대한 조치는 TEPS관리위원회의 처리규정에 따라 이루어집니다.

2. 부정행위 및 규정위반 행위는 현장 적발 뿐만 아니라 사후에도 적발될 수 있으며 모두 동일한 조치가 취해집니다.

3. 부정행위 적발 시 당해 성적은 무효 처리되며 사안에 따라 최대 5년까지 TEPS관리위원회에서 주관하는 모든 시험의 응시자격이 제한됩니다.

4. 문제지 이외에 메모를 하는 행위와 시험 문제의 일부 또는 전부를 유출하거나 공개하는 경우 부정행위로 처리됩니다.

5. 각 파트별 시간을 준수하지 않거나, 시험 종료 후 답안 작성을 계속할 경우 규정위반으로 처리됩니다.

성명 영문 / 시험명

학력

학	졸업 / 재학중	전공	직업
초등학교	○ ○	인문학	공무원
중학교	○ ○	사회과학·법학	고시준비
고등학교	○ ○	경제학·경영학	교사
전문대학	○ ○	자연과학	군인
대학	○ ○	어학·역학·간호학	의료인
대학원	○ ○	공학	자영업
기타	○ ○	약학	학생
		음악·미술·체육	회사원
		기타	공무원
			기타

직종 / 직책

직종	직책
무역	임원
외환	부장
금융	차장
공업 / 공무(과학·공학)	과장
전문직(교직)	대리
전문직(법률·회계·금융)	계장
기술 / 품질관리	사원
영업	보조
홍보 / 광고	무직
총무 / 인사 / 경영	기타
인사 / 서비스 / 비서	
경리 / 회계	
기획	
구매	

단체구분

학생 ○   일반 ○

질문란

1. 귀하의 TEPS 응시목적은?
   ⓐ 입사지원 ⓑ 인사정책
   ⓒ 개인실력측정 ⓓ 입시
   ⓔ 국가고시 자원 ⓕ 기타

2. 귀하의 영어권 체류 경험은?
   ⓐ 없다 ⓑ 6개월 미만
   ⓒ 6개월 이상 1년 미만 ⓓ 1년 이상 3년 미만
   ⓔ 3년 이상 5년 미만 ⓕ 5년 이상

3. 귀하께서 응시하고 계신 고사장에 대한 만족도는?
   ⓐ 0점 ⓑ 1점
   ⓒ 2점 ⓓ 3점
   ⓔ 4점 ⓕ 5점

4. 최근 2년내 TEPS 응시횟수는?
   ⓐ 없다 ⓑ 1회
   ⓒ 2회 ⓓ 3회
   ⓔ 4회 ⓕ 5회 이상

성 명 (성·이름순으로 기재)

HONG   GIL   DONG

(A~Z 마킹표)

뒷면(Side2)

Answer Keys_TEST 1

Listening Comprehension

1 (d)	2 (a)	3 (d)	4 (c)	5 (d)	6 (d)	7 (d)	8 (a)	9 (d)	10 (b)
11 (b)	12 (d)	13 (c)	14 (b)	15 (d)	16 (a)	17 (d)	18 (c)	19 (a)	20 (a)
21 (c)	22 (a)	23 (b)	24 (d)	25 (b)	26 (c)	27 (c)	28 (d)	29 (a)	30 (b)
31 (a)	32 (a)	33 (b)	34 (c)	35 (b)	36 (b)	37 (c)	38 (d)	39 (b)	40 (b)

Vocabulary

1 (c)	2 (c)	3 (a)	4 (a)	5 (b)	6 (b)	7 (c)	8 (b)	9 (c)	10 (a)
11 (a)	12 (a)	13 (d)	14 (b)	15 (a)	16 (d)	17 (c)	18 (a)	19 (d)	20 (d)
21 (b)	22 (b)	23 (a)	24 (b)	25 (b)	26 (c)	27 (b)	28 (b)	29 (a)	30 (c)

Grammar

1 (b)	2 (c)	3 (a)	4 (a)	5 (c)	6 (b)	7 (c)	8 (b)	9 (d)	10 (b)
11 (b)	12 (c)	13 (c)	14 (d)	15 (c)	16 (a)	17 (a)	18 (c)	19 (d)	20 (d)
21 (d)	22 (c)	23 (c)	24 (a)	25 (d)	26 (c)	27 (b)	28 (d)	29 (c)	30 (c)

Reading Comprehension

1 (b)	2 (a)	3 (b)	4 (a)	5 (b)	6 (b)	7 (d)	8 (b)	9 (d)	10 (b)
11 (a)	12 (c)	13 (d)	14 (c)	15 (c)	16 (b)	17 (a)	18 (c)	19 (d)	20 (b)
21 (d)	22 (d)	23 (a)	24 (d)	25 (c)	26 (c)	27 (d)	28 (b)	29 (d)	30 (c)
31 (d)	32 (d)	33 (d)	34 (d)	35 (d)					

독점 출간

가장 최신 텝스 기출 문제를 수록한

서울대 텝스 관리위원회
텝스 최신기출
1200제 시리즈

서울대 텝스 관리위원회
텝스 최신기출 1200제
문제집/해설집 1

서울대 텝스 관리위원회
텝스 최신기출 1200제
문제집/해설집 2

서울대 텝스 관리위원회
텝스 최신기출 1200제
문제집/해설집 3

서울대 텝스 관리위원회 최신 기출 문제는 넥서스에서 **독점 출간**합니다.

NEW TEPS 실전 모의고사 3회분

지은이 김무룡, 넥서스 TEPS연구소
펴낸이 임상진
펴낸곳 (주)넥서스

초판 1쇄 발행 2018년 5월 25일
초판 9쇄 발행 2024년 5월 1일

출판신고 1992년 4월 3일 제311-2002-2호
10880 경기도 파주시 지목로 5
Tel (02)330-5500 Fax (02)330-5555

ISBN 979-11-6165-317-4 13740

저자와 출판사의 허락 없이 내용의 일부를 인용하거나
발췌하는 것을 금합니다.

가격은 뒤표지에 있습니다.
잘못 만들어진 책은 구입처에서 바꾸어 드립니다.

www.nexusbook.com

NEW TEPS 실전 모의고사

새롭게 바뀐 NEW TEPS를 대비하는 실전 모의고사

★ 서울대텝스관리위원회 NEW TEPS 경향 완벽 반영

★ 실제 NEW TEPS 시험지 그대로 구성한 실전 모의고사 3회분 수록

★ 청해 스크립트 및 쉽고 자세한 해석/해설 온라인 무료 다운로드 제공

★ NEW TEPS 실전용·복습용·고사장 버전의 3종 MP3 무료 다운로드

★ 청취력 향상을 위한 온라인/모바일 받아쓰기 테스트 제공

QR코드 / www.nexusbook.com

MP3를 가장 빠르고 쉽게 듣는 방법

❶ 구글 플레이, 앱스토어에서 "콜롬북스" 어플 설치
❷ 도서명으로 검색
❸ 실전용, 복습용, 고사장 버전 3종 MP3 다운로드

MP3 바로 듣기
해석·해설 확인
받아쓰기 테스트

TEST 2

TEPS

Test of English Proficiency
developed by
Seoul National University

NEW TEPS 시험 구성

영역	문제 유형	문항수	제한 시간	점수 범위
청해 Listening Comprehension	Part I : 한 문장을 듣고 이어질 대화로 가장 적절한 답 고르기 (문장 1회 청취 후 선택지 1회 청취)	10	40분	0~240점
	Part II : 짧은 대화를 듣고 이어질 대화로 가장 적절한 답 고르기 (대화 1회 청취 후 선택지 1회 청취)	10		
	Part III : 긴 대화를 듣고 질문에 가장 적절한 답 고르기 (대화 및 질문 1회 청취 후 선택지 1회 청취)	10		
	Part IV : 담화를 듣고 질문에 가장 적절한 답 고르기(1지문 1문항) (담화 및 질문 2회 청취 후 선택지 1회 청취)	6		
	신유형 Part V : 담화를 듣고 질문에 가장 적절한 답 고르기(1지문 2문항) (담화 및 질문 2회 청취 후 선택지 1회 청취)	4		
어휘 Vocabulary	Part I : 대화문의 빈칸에 가장 적절한 어휘 고르기	10	통합 25분	0~60점
	Part II : 단문의 빈칸에 가장 적절한 어휘 고르기	20		
문법 Grammar	Part I : 대화문의 빈칸에 가장 적절한 답 고르기	10		0~60점
	Part II : 단문의 빈칸에 가장 적절한 답 고르기	15		
	Part III : 대화 및 문단에서 문법상 틀리거나 어색한 부분 고르기	5		
독해 Reading Comprehension	Part I : 지문을 읽고 빈칸에 가장 적절한 답 고르기	10	40분	0~240점
	Part II : 지문을 읽고 문맥상 어색한 내용 고르기	2		
	Part III : 지문을 읽고 질문에 가장 적절한 답 고르기(1지문 1문항)	13		
	신유형 Part IV : 지문을 읽고 질문에 가장 적절한 답 고르기(1지문 2문항)	10		
총계	14개 Parts	135문항	105분	0~600점

TEPS

Listening Comprehension

Directions

1. In the Listening Comprehension section, all content will be presented orally rather than in written form.

2. This section contains five parts. For each part, you will receive separate instructions. Listen to the instructions carefully, and choose the best answer from the options for each item.

MP3 바로 듣기
해석·해설 확인
받아쓰기 테스트

Part I Questions 1~10

You will now hear ten individual spoken questions or statements, each followed by four spoken responses. Choose the most appropriate response for each item.

Part II Questions 11~20

You will now hear ten short conversation fragments, each followed by four spoken responses. Choose the most appropriate response to complete each conversation.

Part III **Questions 21~30**

You will now hear ten complete conversations. For each conversation, you will be asked to answer a question. Before each conversation, you will hear a short description of the situation. After listening to the description and conversation once, you will hear a question and four options. Based on the given information, choose the option that best answers the question.

Part IV Questions 31~36

You will now hear six short talks. After each talk, you will be asked to answer a question. Each talk and its corresponding question will be read twice. Then you will hear four options which will be read only once. Based on the given information, choose the option that best answers the question.

Part V Questions 37~40

You will now hear two longer talks. After each talk, you will be asked to answer two questions. Each talk and its corresponding questions will be read twice. However, the four options for each question will be read only once. Based on the given information, choose the option that best answers each question.

TEPS

Vocabulary & Grammar

Directions

These two sections test your vocabulary and grammar knowledge. You will have 25 minutes to complete a total of 60 questions: 30 from the Vocabulary section and 30 from the Grammar section. Be sure to follow the directions given by the proctor.

Part I Questions 1~10

Choose the option that best completes each dialogue.

1. A: Let's see, you could come over tomorrow at 8.
   B: OK, but I'll check my _____ first.
   (a) mobility
   (b) schemer
   (c) itinerary
   (d) ancillary

2. A: This painting is a masterpiece, don't you think?
   B: Absolutely, it's made a(n) _____ impression on me.
   (a) tepid
   (b) balmy
   (c) devious
   (d) indelible

3. A: We shouldn't have invested in that company. We lost a lot.
   B: I know. It will be a _____ amount.
   (a) rugged
   (b) residual
   (c) collective
   (d) substantial

4. A: Brenda always has her homework done on time.
   B: Yes, she's very _____.
   (a) benign
   (b) diligent
   (c) generous
   (d) compelling

5. A: Are you sure this is the road to the highway?
   B: Well, I'm not entirely _____.
   (a) alert
   (b) mindful
   (c) positive
   (d) fathomable

6. A: Excuse me, sir, I need to check your luggage.
   B: Oh, I'm sure you'll find everything in _____.
   (a) safe
   (b) order
   (c) reason
   (d) course

7. A: Are you sure you can manage this task?
   B: Sure, I think I am _____ enough.
   (a) rustic
   (b) competent
   (c) extraneous
   (d) fundamental

8. A: Are you sure you don't have time to go skiing?
   B: I'm sorry, I'm _____ these days.
   (a) flat out
   (b) flung up
   (c) stuck up
   (d) strung out

9. A: Which way is it to the pharmacy?
   B: Not sure, but it's in the _____.
   (a) plot
   (b) terrain
   (c) vicinity
   (d) environment

10. A: Hi, this is Brad calling. Is Jenny Black at that address?
    B: Sorry, she no longer _____ here.
    (a) homes
    (b) adopts
    (c) resides
    (d) partakes

Part II Questions 11~30

Choose the option that best completes each sentence.

11. Increasing calcium intake is a common _____ for reducing bone fractures, but vitamin D is also important to help the body utilize calcium.

    (a) malice
    (b) license
    (c) strategy
    (d) aggravation

12. The _____ of tech vendors creates a crowded marketplace, where vendors and their products start to all seem the same.

    (a) deck
    (b) glut
    (c) adage
    (d) bubble

13. Henry VIII fully believed that the social order of England had to be _____ at all costs and so he resisted any change.

    (a) locked
    (b) hedged
    (c) bracketed
    (d) maintained

14. Reindeer in arctic regions have a different internal clock from the one that drives the daily biological _____ in other organisms.

    (a) waves
    (b) genres
    (c) rhythms
    (d) draughts

15. The Romantic Circles Web site is the _____ product of editors, contributors, and users worldwide with a shared interest in the art of the Romantic era.

    (a) stilted
    (b) adjacent
    (c) erroneous
    (d) collaborative

16. Scientists can now _____ between healthy cells and cancer cells, whereas in the past they could not tell them apart.

    (a) allure
    (b) refract
    (c) extinguish
    (d) discern

17. On Monday night, the Rock and Roll Hall of Fame will welcome its latest _____ at New York's Waldorf Astoria hotel.

    (a) crafts
    (b) novices
    (c) vestiges
    (d) inductees

18. Conventional biodiesel production _____ plant oils and then converts them into fatty acid esters that can be used to power engines.

    (a) lists
    (b) daubs
    (c) rustles
    (d) extracts

19. Hitler's mother had _____ on her son, and for the rest of his life Hitler carried a photo of her wherever he went.

    (a) hoed
    (b) doted
    (c) blighted
    (d) harangued

20. In Africa, many pregnant and lactating women obtain _____ they need by eating forms of clay.

    (a) residues
    (b) nutrients
    (c) mediums
    (d) applause

21. Depression becomes an illness when symptoms intensify and _____ over an extended period of time.

    (a) falter
    (b) dilute
    (c) persist
    (d) replenish

22. Analysts feel that the US economy could _____ and recover sooner than expect.

    (a) polish
    (b) adhere
    (c) rebound
    (d) decimate

23. The latest round of government data on worker _____ indicates that people are working harder for less pay.

    (a) luster
    (b) ridicule
    (c) diversion
    (d) productivity

24. For over thirty years, the Bermuda Triangle has been popularly known for supposedly _____ disappearances of boats and aircraft.

    (a) naughty
    (b) awkward
    (c) illustrious
    (d) paranormal

25. Sir Frank Whittle was the man that designed the first practical jet engine in the 1920's and _____ the way people traveled.

    (a) branded
    (b) endured
    (c) revolved
    (d) transformed

26. The 10 kilometer wide meteor that struck near modern-day Mexico 65 million years ago _____ doom for the dinosaurs and many other species.

    (a) noticed
    (b) spelled
    (c) laundered
    (d) conformed

27. New technology involving silicon nano wires could _____ the power of lithium-ion batteries by as much as a factor of 10.

    (a) tick
    (b) boost
    (c) harass
    (d) resume

28. It has long been assumed that sleep deprivation can create _____ with our emotions and new research now proves why this is true.

    (a) jest
    (b) havoc
    (c) riddle
    (d) seizure

29. In the new book, the author _____ the importance placed upon money and health by the characters of Jane Austen's novels.

    (a) rakes
    (b) disjoins
    (c) caresses
    (d) scrutinizes

30. The unregulated nature of the Web has aided a _____ of cyber-hate on personal blogs as well as mainstream social-networking sites.

    (a) toil
    (b) brigade
    (c) fragment
    (d) proliferation

You have finished the Vocabulary questions. Please continue on to the Grammar questions.

Part I Questions 1~10

Choose the option that best completes each dialogue.

1. A: Will this cleaner be good enough for the bathroom?
   B: Yes, that cleaner _____.
   (a) well works
   (b) is well working
   (c) works quite well
   (d) is quite working well

2. A: You won the race! See, I knew you were a great athlete.
   B: But if you hadn't coached me, I _____ probably come in last.
   (a) can have
   (b) would have
   (c) should have
   (d) ought to have

3. A: How do I get the program I want on cable?
   B: Here, I'll show you how _____ the remote.
   (a) operating
   (b) to operate
   (c) for operating
   (d) is being operated

4. A: Ron says he will quit trying to make a singing career.
   B: But he is _____ to just give up like that.
   (a) talented singer
   (b) singer too talented
   (c) too talented a singer
   (d) really talented singer

5. A: How is Leonie doing in Europe, do you know?
   B: Actually, we _____ to hear from her today.
   (a) are expecting
   (b) will have expected
   (c) would be expecting
   (d) should have been expected

6. A: So, do you think you'll get first prize for your essay?
   B: No, I'm not _____ presumptuous.
   (a) so
   (b) such
   (c) a lot
   (d) most

7. A: What did the doctor say about Peter's pills?
   B: It's recommended he _____ one before each meal.
   (a) take
   (b) takes
   (c) is taking
   (d) has taken

8. A: Why did you want to talk to me about Geoffrey?
   B: I just wanted to give you _____ piece of advice.
   (a) a
   (b) the
   (c) each
   (d) other

9. A: Are you feeling better today?
   B: _____ a good night's sleep, I feel great.
   (a) I had
   (b) Having
   (d) To have
   (d) Having had

10. A: I wish I could speak English fluently.
    B: Me too, but _____ to speak it well.
    (a) to me is difficult
    (b) I'm really difficult
    (c) it's really difficult
    (d) really difficult to me

Part II Questions 11~25

Choose the option that best completes each sentence.

11. Workers learn to behave in a certain fashion through demonstrations or the process of _____ behavior they observe.

    (a) imitate
    (b) imitating
    (c) to imitate
    (d) being imitated

12. With the economy experiencing a downturn, the company CEO realized that it _____ necessary to lay-off some workers.

    (a) be
    (b) is being
    (c) would be
    (d) will have been

13. Though employees were worried about the new manager, they soon found him _____ to get along with.

    (a) easy person
    (b) an easy person
    (c) the easy person
    (d) some easy person

14. During the chase, a police car _____ by several bullets and the car broke down as a result.

    (a) had hit
    (b) was hit
    (c) had been hitting
    (d) has been being hit

15. Everyone heard from David about his boss _____ insisted everything be done on time.

    (a) who
    (b) where
    (c) in what
    (d) for whom

16. One of several computers, along with boxes of documents, notebooks, and files, _____ by the FBI during the raid.

    (a) having took
    (b) will take
    (c) was taken
    (d) were taken

17. The family's German shepherd always _____ a leash when he goes out for walks in the park.

    (a) wore
    (b) wears
    (c) had worn
    (d) was wearing

18. The language student had to translate _____ and it took him hours to do it.

    (a) in English long and difficult passage
    (b) a long, difficult passage into English
    (c) long and a difficult passage of English
    (d) into English passage long and difficult

19. The Grand Modus is an extremely refined car, _____ low running costs, decent fuel economy, low insurance costs and cheap servicing.

    (a) combines
    (b) combining
    (c) to combine
    (d) it combines

20. _____ the Henry James novel for class, the student looked forward to an easier novel to read.

    (a) Finished finally
    (b) He finally finished
    (c) Had finally finished
    (d) Having finally finished

21. It is estimated that if everything goes to plan, the construction project should be completed _____ six months.

    (a) at
    (b) in
    (c) for
    (d) until

22. There is a compelling case for educating the public about science _____ they better understand its goals, methods and benefits.

    (a) though
    (b) so that
    (c) because
    (d) but also

23. During the Black Death of 1348, _____ bring the sick what they asked for or watch over them when they were dying.

    (a) least did people do else
    (b) people did little more than
    (c) a little could people do than
    (d) not other people could do but

24. The woman shopping for antiques was delighted to find a _____ vase that was over 200 years old.

    (a) nice small cream-colored porcelain
    (b) cream-colored nice porcelain small
    (c) porcelain cream-colored small nice
    (d) small cream-colored nice porcelain

25. Dubai's population has soared in recent years as expatriates, _____ by the country, continue to arrive in the region for work.

    (a) courted
    (b) for courting
    (c) they are courted
    (d) have been courted

Part III Questions 26~30

Read each dialogue or passage carefully and identify the option that contains a grammatical error.

26. (a) A: Studying has become so expensive these days, don't you think?
    (b) B: Yeah, more and more of students are having to take out loans.
    (c) A: That's exactly what I might have to do. I can't make ends meet.
    (d) B: Well, I'm OK for now, but only because I've got a part time job.

27. (a) A: I've got tickets to a baseball game. Are you interested in them?
    (b) B: I'm not a big fan of baseball. I really don't know much about it.
    (c) A: Actually, same here. Baseball is not very interesting to watch it.
    (d) B: Hey, I bet my brother would want the tickets. He follows baseball.

28. (a) In a few weeks, the government of British Colombia will allow the hunting of bears in the internationally celebrated Great Bear Rainforest. (b) And the spirit bear, of whom was featured in the Vancouver Olympic Games' opening ceremony, could be one of the targets. (c) But conservationists are protesting the hunt with the release of a full page ad in *the Vancouver Sun*. (d) The ad is supported by over 20 million people, who are appalled that Canadian spirit bears will be hunted.

29. (a) A washing machine for dogs is proving to be a boon for pet owners in Japan whose pets shun a traditional bath. (b) The "dog wash" was designed in the US and gives pets an automatic drenching with warm water and then a blow-dry. (c) While some dogs remain calm in the machine compartment, others are scared and upset at being washed. (d) Even more disturbing, people put cats in the washer, which is stupid idea because most cats hate water.

30. (a) Political sensation Wayne Rogers is confident in his ability as a 19-year-old university student to contest a political election. (b) He was picked this weekend as the Liberal Party's best hope for winning a marginal seat at this year's federal election. (c) But his pre-selection was a flashpoint for growing discontent within the federal ranks of the Liberal Party. (d) The decision has only been fueled existing anger over some of the local Liberal Party hierarchy's decision-making.

You have reached the end of the Vocabulary & Grammar sections. Do NOT move on to the Reading Comprehension section until instructed to do so. You are NOT allowed to turn to any other section of the test.

Reading Comprehension

TEPS

DIRECTIONS

This section tests your ability to comprehend reading passages. You will have 40 minutes to complete 35 questions. Be sure to follow the directions given by the proctor.

Part I Questions 1~10

Read the passage and choose the option that best completes the passage.

1. Designtech is an industry leader in providing branding, marketing and architecture services to the financial community. We are experiencing growth in our San Francisco office. We now seek candidates registered as CA architects with a minimum of 10 years experience. This position requires knowledge of programming, ability to design through design development, coordination of projects from document phase through to construction. Must have _____. Excellent written and oral communication skills are also required. We offer very competitive salary plus benefits. Send résumé to douglas.thomas@designtech.com.

    (a) real-estate and marketing experience
    (b) creative design and drafting software skills
    (c) building tradesman licenses and qualifications
    (d) excellent track record in home sales management

2. Once thought of as more of a mental problem, it turns out that chronic feelings of loneliness take a toll on blood pressure over time. Research into this issue can now show this through a direct relation between loneliness and larger increases in blood pressure four years later. This link is independent of age standards and other factors that could cause blood pressure to rise, including body-mass index, smoking, alcohol use and demographic differences such as race and income. What this means is that loneliness _____.

    (a) is a unique health-risk factor in its own right
    (b) has more detrimental effects the more one ages
    (c) can cause a whole range of mental health problems
    (d) contributes to high blood pressure but it is negligible

3. Soil respiration is when plants and microbes in the soil give off carbon dioxide. According to a 20 year analysis, this soil respiration has increased about one-tenth of 1 percent per year since 1989. The analysis also revealed that the total amount of carbon dioxide flowing from soils is about 10-15 percent higher than previous measurements. This big amount of carbon dioxide coming off of the surface of the soil everywhere in the world does appear to be in response to a rise in temperature. It is not at the moment greatly affecting the greenhouse effect. Nonetheless, climate change is _____.

    (a) affecting the behavior of these microbes
    (b) increasing carbon dioxide release from soil
    (c) definitely on the rise according to the scientists
    (d) less of a factor in soil respiration than once thought

4. Business plans for investors are usually about 20 pages long and must be grounded in a deep knowledge of your industry and the money-making opportunities within it. But if you think you only need a business plan for going after capital, you are wrong. A business plan, thoughtfully assembled and diligently updated, should be regarded as your company blueprint. It sets direction, facilitates communication and establishes performance metrics. Well-articulated business plans force business owners to constantly weigh the strengths and weaknesses of their operations. So, a business plan _____.

(a) should not be long and over complicated
(b) should focus on attracting investor capital
(c) is not just for courting professional investors
(d) is important but not as much as a profit model

5. In his short life, author Anton Chekhov published more than 500 stories, but there was a lot more to this man, not to mention plays that are masterpieces of drama, and his work as a doctor until the last stages of his fatal illness. He was indeed a man of multiple talents. In the new release *Stories of Chekhov*, we are reminded of this story after story. It is a book that is not just about Chekhov's mastery of the short story form. Each story offers a great deal more. The introductions, with their original commentaries, _____.

(a) have been brilliantly translated from the Russian
(b) explain his short storytelling techniques in detail
(c) provide insights into many facets of Chekhov's life
(d) focus exclusively on Chekhov's dramatic masterpieces

6. A doctor assesses the risks in performing a necessary transplant based on several factors, including the status of your disease and your health. A disease can change over time. If a disease is stable or in remission, a transplant is viable, but if it is becoming chronic, a transplant would be unwise. Similarly, your general health must also be considered. For example, if you have liver or kidney damage, it creates a risk factor. However, when you are healthy, and your organs work well, _____.

   (a) you are less likely to catch disease
   (b) a transplant is more likely to go well
   (c) your chance of kidney damage is lower
   (d) a doctor would not perform a transplant

7. My parents and I suffered a lot in Paris from June 14, 1940, to May 8, 1945, during the German occupation. After the Germans entered Paris, we lacked everything and it lasted more than 5 years. We had to scrounge for food and we were often hungry and cold. I remember that fateful day when it all began, June 14, 1940, the day of the entry of the German army. Even till the day before, Parisians were saying it would never happen. But on the 14 June, it did. I will never forget that day, as I stood and watched _____.

   (a) our home and possessions taken from us
   (b) gangs of Frenchmen fighting in the streets
   (c) soldiers parading through Paris in great numbers
   (d) people begging for food because they were hungry

8.
   ### Science Report

   New research on mice shows that natural purple pigments in fruits, vegetables and berries may help prevent obesity. The pigments in question are the ones responsible for the darker colors blue, purple and red of certain fruits, such as berries and vegetables. However, researchers also found that eating the whole fruit containing the pigments was less effective than eating an extract of a berry. Pigments fed to mice by way of a whole blueberry, for example, did not prevent and may have actually increased obesity. However, the opposite is true _____.

   (a) if using strawberry rather than blueberry pigment
   (b) when the research was conducted on humans
   (c) if vegetables rather than fruit were fed to mice
   (d) when mice were given a purified form of pigment

9. India is a growing destination for innovative activities by multinational companies and this manifests itself in the form of a growing presence of foreign research and development centers. Foreign direct investment also has been steadily increasing and during 2009 there were a number of high-profile takeovers of western technology-based companies by Indian corporations. _____, analysts continued to think tough times were around the corner for India because of the global financial crisis. Upward growth performance, however, has continued unabated and proved them wrong.

   (a) Additionally
   (b) Because of this
   (c) Notwithstanding
   (d) Put another way

10. If you damage your Acme boat propeller, it is easy to have it repaired. Even though Acme propellers have a unique look, they are repaired much the same way as any other propeller. _____, it is not possible to return an Acme propeller to perfectly new condition because that would require maintaining blades to plus or minus the thickness of a human hair. But Acme propellers are built with such accuracy and consistency that it means blade thicknesses, for example, is consistent on each blade, which makes propellers easier to repair.

    (a) Instead
    (b) What's more
    (c) As can be expected
    (d) Under these circumstances

> **Part II** **Questions 11~12**
>
> Read the passage and identify the option that does NOT belong.

11. Over the past year, scientists have found convincing evidence that the moon holds significant amounts of water. (a) Until now, most research has concentrated on the ice within deep, dark craters near the south pole. (b) Evidence from radar signals bounced off the moon's surface by India's Chandrayaan-1 moon probe indicates water ice. (c) Now efforts concentrating on the north pole have revealed that within 40 small craters is an estimated 600 million metric tons of water. (d) That is significant because the ice in these craters could be used by future lunar explorers for drinking or creating oxygen.

12. Cherry blossoms can be viewed from mid-January through June in different regions in Japan. (a) People enjoy having picnics under cherry trees, which is a custom called a hanami or viewing party. (b) These beautiful flowers are indigenous to many countries in East Asia and come in a wide number of varieties. (c) However, the period of blooming in any one area only lasts for a short time, sometimes just for a week. (d) So when the cherry blossoms are out, people fill the parks in great numbers and to see them before it is too late.

Part III **Questions 13~25**

Read the passage, question, and options. Then, based on the given information, choose the option that best answers each question.

13.
> **Notice**
>
> There are lots of problems caused by temperature drop in winter.
> Here are some things you should check to stay warm:
>
> · When the temperature goes below -10 degrees Celsius, make sure that you turn your heaters on.
>
> · Cover the water meter with warm blankets.
>
> · Let all faucets drip to prevent freezing of the water inside the pipe. If your water pipe has frozen, it can burst and cause major problems.
>
> · It is best to remove the snow around door entrances as soon as possible when it is snowy. The snow might turn into ice after some time.
>
> Please remember that being cautious can make you warm at your own home.
> If you need help, contact the Repair and Management office.

Q: What is the main purpose of the notice?
(a) To warn residents about a burst in the water pipe
(b) To advise residents on how to get through the cold winter
(c) To remind residents to use heaters cautiously
(d) To inform residents of the upcoming renovation

14. Pieces of ceramic can be the raw material for art. That is how to look at them when creating a mosaic. First collect all the ceramic pieces of the colors you want. Then, purchase the appropriate adhesive and tile grout. Place your ceramic pieces in a pattern on the surface you want to decorate, such as a flowerpot or table top. Glue each piece in place. When dry, apply tile grout to the gaps between pieces with a putty knife or rubber-gloved fingers. Wipe off any excess and wait for the grout to dry. Your work of art is done!

Q: What are the instructions mainly about?
(a) Making artworks from raw materials
(b) Overlaying art work with ceramic pieces
(c) Creating a decorative ceramic mosaic
(d) Designing patterns for ceramic objects

15. Whether unrealized educational expectations are associated with depression among adults is a question that various studies have addressed. One study found no long-term emotional costs of aiming high and falling short when it comes to educational aspirations, despite psychological theories that suggest otherwise. Negative mental health outcomes were more likely from not trying. In addition, trying may lead to higher achievements and the mental and material benefits that go along with them. That study's conclusion was that society should not discourage unpromising students who have dreams of earning a college degree.

Q: What is the main point about education in the passage?
(a) Depression in adults is not related to a poor education.
(b) Unrealized expectations in university do incur depression.
(c) Poor education standards can have a psychological impact.
(d) Aiming high and failing is not consequential for mental health.

16. A new tool for collecting chemical or biological samples is now available. It is a sampler gun that eliminates direct contact with anything harmful, as well as any risk of contaminating evidence in the case of investigation of a crime scene. Traditional ways of gathering samples use many gadgets. This device puts several technologies into one, easy-to-use gun. It has a cotton pad that grabs chemicals, a GPS system to record the samples' location, a camera that snaps pictures for evidence, and a digital voice recorder and writing pad for taking notes. The tool is ideal for all kinds of forensic biology applications.

Q: What is the main idea about the new tool in the passage?
(a) It has a useful gun shape design for collecting samples.
(b) It is an evidence-gathering machine to use at crime scenes.
(c) It makes investigative sampling hands-off, easier and risk free.
(d) It more accurately finds samples thanks to superior technology.

17.

> ### Unique Earrings for Women
>
> Add a sparkle to your wardrobe with these five sterling silver earrings, featuring five different colored gems. This set makes a great gift—each set of stud earrings is packaged in a separate metallic blue gift box. All five boxes come packaged together with a metallic blue stand to hold the boxes together, though they can be easily separated. With this set, you can more closely match the colors of your clothes. You can wear a different pair of earrings for each day of the work week! And the entire set has a total carat weight of 8.25 carats.

Q: Which of the following is correct according to the advertisement?
(a) Earrings can be either silver or gem colored.
(b) Five colored gems feature on a pair of sterling earrings.
(c) Stud pairs are contained in individual gift boxes.
(d) Many earring set color combinations can be chosen.

18. Two of the most famous leaders from the later Roman Empire were Constantine the Great and Julian the Apostate. Yet they were opposites in their approach to religion. Constantine was the first Christian Roman emperor, and in 313 he announced toleration of Christianity by law, thus setting Christianity in place in the Roman Empire. Julian, who became emperor in 355, was the last non-Christian ruler of the Roman Empire. He tried to reverse the trend toward Christianity, hoping to bring the empire back to its ancient Roman values and to reintegrate Hellenistic paganism. He did not succeed and Christianity continued to grow.

Q: Which of the following is correct according to the passage?
(a) Constantine's rule as emperor abruptly ended in 313.
(b) Julian and Constantine fought each other over religion.
(c) Constantine became the last Christian ruler over Rome.
(d) Julian desired to make paganism a part of Roman society.

19. John Neumeier's ballet adaptation of "The Little Mermaid" is infused with stark blue and white light, angular movements, expressionistic visual imagery, and is often nightmarish. For audiences weaned on the peppy 1989 Walt Disney animated film version of *The Little Mermaid*, this is a bleak take on Hans Christian Andersen's 1837 fairy tale. Mr. Neumeier's version of Andersen's cautionary tale about a young woman who risks everything for love is typical of what we see these days. Artists are adapting long-established children's works for stage and screen but focusing too much on the dark aspects of the tales.

Q: What has John Neumeier done with "The Little Mermaid?"
(a) He rewrote it to make it less about a mermaid.
(b) He followed an earlier Disney version too closely.
(c) He recast it in order to create a nightmarish vision.
(d) He lightened up some of its harsh and darker aspects.

20. In recent years Peruvian and international researchers have discovered over 4,000 cave paintings and rock carvings in different areas of Peru. These artistic representations date from 8,000 BC to the arrival of the first Spanish Conquistadors in the 16th century. The most ancient sites show a predominance of naturalistic representations of hunting and animals. However, more recent sites, dated at 4,000 to 5,000 years BC, depict fertility rather than hunting. This stylistic development coincides with the beginnings of pastoralism and symbolizes the change in man-animal relationships that accompanied it.

Q: Which of the following is correct according to the passage?
(a) Four thousand ancient carvings were found in Peru.
(b) The earliest Peruvian cave art dates back to 4,000 BC.
(c) Ancient Peruvian art consists of some naturalistic images.
(d) The idea of fertility appears throughout ancient Peruvian art.

21.

News Report

A 29-year-old man has been hospitalized with serious burns following a powerful explosion and fire Sunday night at a restaurant in Bedford. The sound and force of the explosion startled residents up to three kilometers away and brought them to the scene, where they found the man outside the restaurant. The restaurant was razed by the explosion and fire. Damage to other businesses occurred from flying debris and the shock of the blast. Fire crews and police investigating the incident suspect arson, since it is the third time the building has been damaged by fire in the past two years.

Q: Which of the following is correct according to the news report?
(a) Restaurant patrons were caught in a serious fire.
(b) A Bedford explosion attracted residents from afar.
(c) Businesses sustained fire damage from an explosion.
(d) A suspected arsonist was apprehended by Bedford police.

22. According to historical accounts, Iceland was known to Irish monks in the latter part of the 8th century, who used to sail there. However, actual settlement of Iceland began with the Vikings in 874. A Viking named Ingolfur Arnarson is recorded as the first settler. He was a chieftain from Norway who arrived in Iceland with his family and dependants in 874. He started a farm in Reykjavik, which later became the country's capital. The years between 874 and 930 saw increasing numbers of Viking settlers who arrived from Scandinavia and claimed land in the inhabitable areas.

Q: Which of the following is correct about Iceland's first Vikings?
(a) They arrived in Reykjavik in the late 8th century.
(b) They settled Iceland prior to the arrival of Irish monks.
(c) They fled from Iceland with a chieftain called Arnarson.
(d) They preceded later Vikings who were from Scandinavia.

23.

To the Editor:

Your editorial of March 17, "It Starts with Good Teachers" is typical of society's attitude towards teachers. We are used to getting either demonized because we are responsible for all the ills of our society, or else patronized by being told that there must be some good ones among us. It was amazing to see *The Examiner* express both clichés in one editorial. Teachers are always heartened to know that at the moment when the educational system is being de-funded, they can be expected to improve performance and achieve magic. Clearly, *The Examiner* needs an education.

Philip Crinkle

Q: What can be inferred about the writer from the letter?
(a) He has a poor grasp of the education system.
(b) He is disgruntled by the performance of teachers.
(c) He is unimpressed by false perceptions of teachers.
(d) He believes teachers can achieve a lot without funding.

24. The author of *A Lone Writer*, the biography of writer Nathan Alger, is far from subtle in her approach. Author Dorothy Mead will make you wince on almost every page. To hear her tell Alger's story is like listening to a coarse gossip monger. This book's tone—narrated as if by a waitress in a cheap diner—isn't improved by Mead's referring to people by their nicknames. She even calls Nathan Alger's fans a bunch of "loons, cripples, permanent deadbeats and retards." Worse by far are Mead's dismal readings of Alger's novels. She has no feeling for his work at all.

Q: What can be inferred from the review?
(a) Mead's biography suits Alger's reputation.
(b) Little can be recommended of Mead's book.
(c) Alger's writings would not be enjoyable to read.
(d) Though unsubtle, Mead's assessment is accurate.

25.

THE NORTHVILLE TIMES

New State Policy

In order to make sure cars are not emitting a lot of pollution, states will allow private repair shops to conduct both safety and emissions tests simultaneously. This will make it easier for car owners to renew their car licenses. However, some people think dishonest repair shops will make customers fail an emissions test so they have to pay for repairs. But the risk is that a customer might buy a new car. That is no good for the repair business. So, shops might actually cheat by helping people pass, whose vehicles are older and need regular mechanical repairs.

Q: What can be inferred about the new state policy?
(a) It gives repair shops less incentive to cheat.
(b) It might not lower pollution as much as anticipated.
(c) It will ensure people take emission tests more often.
(d) It is likely to result in newer cars being on the roads.

Part IV Questions 26~35

Read the passage, questions, and options. Then, based on the given information, choose the option that best answers each question.

Questions 26-27

http://www.yummydonut.com/csr/volunteer

| Our Story | Menu | Locations | Order | CSR |

Volunteer to Serve the Disadvantaged

Corporate social responsibility is at the heart of everything we do at Yummy Donut. From the beginning of our company, we have been aware of the effects of what we do on the community we serve. Of course, our primary mission is to serve delicious donuts to customers. At the same time, we firmly believe that a socially responsible company should care about the disadvantaged. That is why we volunteer to feed them for free every two weeks throughout the year.

Some critics accuse us of engaging in "cause-marketing." To begin with, there is nothing wrong with cause-marketing. There are too many worthy causes to pursue, and one company cannot pursue all of them. Furthermore, everyone at Yummy Donut believes in the intrinsic value of serving others. Again, there are too many disadvantaged people we should serve. By feeding some of them for free, we do our bit for a better society.

26. Q: Which of the following is correct according to the passage?

(a) Yummy Donut is a family-owned company based in the United States.
(b) Corporate social responsibility is indispensable to Yummy Donut.
(c) Everyone at Yummy Donut serves primarily for extrinsic rewards.
(d) Every other day, Yummy Donut feeds the disadvantaged free of charge.

27. Q: What can be inferred from the passage?

(a) Corporate social responsibility is a concept developed by Yummy Donut.
(b) Yummy Donut serves tasty donuts to customers on a quarterly basis.
(c) Yummy Donut believes that cause-marketing is an unassailable concept.
(d) Yummy Donut is the only donut company involved in cause-marketing.

Questions 28-29

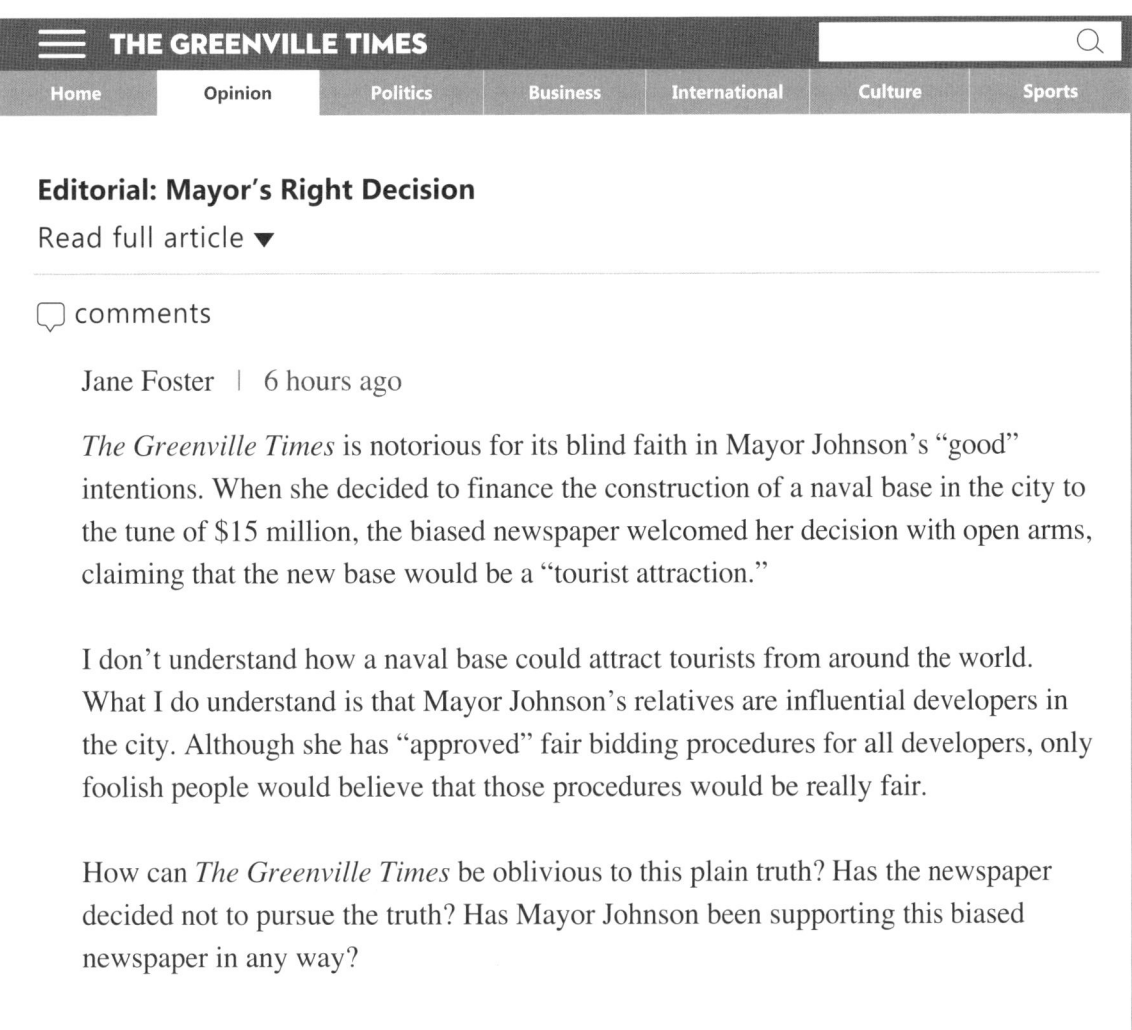

28. Q: What is the main purpose of the passage?

    (a) To criticize the newspaper for naively believing that the naval base would attract large numbers of tourists to Greenville
    (b) To attack the newspaper for endorsing the mayor's decision without considering her motive
    (c) To point out that nepotism remains prevalent under Mayor Johnson
    (d) To encourage the newspaper to pursue the truth no matter what

29. Q: What can be inferred about Foster from the passage?

    (a) She is a regular subscriber to *The Greenville Times*.
    (b) She does not believe that fairness is a signature trait of *The Greenville Times*.
    (c) She has been harboring a grudge against Mayor Johnson since she was elected.
    (d) She will submit bidding documents to the City of Greenville.

Questions 30-31

http://www.realdocu.com/filmfestival/submission

ABOUT | SUBMISSION | WINNERS | VIEWERS | CONTRIBUTION

Guidelines for Submitting Documentary Films

▶ Deadlines and Submission Fees

Early Deadline: May 5, 2018
· Short Films: $100
· American Films: $300
· Canadian Films: $350
· International Films: $200

Official Deadline: June 6, 2018
· Short Films: $150
· American Films: $350
· Canadian Films: $400
· International Films: $250

Submission Policy
· Please note that all international films must be submitted with English subtitles.
· We will not accept any previously submitted films.

Should you have any further questions, please email Emily Smith at emilys@realdocu.com.

30. Q: What would be the submission fee if you submit a Korean film on May 15, 2018?

(a) $150
(b) $200
(c) $250
(d) $300

31. Q: What can be inferred from the guidelines?

(a) The guidelines imply that the submission fee is non-refundable.
(b) If you miss the official deadline, you will be charged a late fee.
(c) Ms. Smith is supposed to forward all inquiries to the film committee.
(d) Those who view submitted films are likely to be fluent in English.

Questions 32-33

Book Review

Everybody's Guide to Natural Cleaners by Susan Black

Susan Black is well-known as "the Mozart of the cleaning industry." She has run a number of successful cleaning companies, from Cleaning Floors to Your #1 Dry Cleaner's. Although she has been highly successful in taking advantage of chemical cleaning products, Black is keenly aware that they are potentially harmful to the environment. That is why she has written this reader-friendly guide to natural cleaners.

Black starts this guide by talking about how her grandmother taught her how to use many different kinds of natural cleaners, including vinegar. In fact, she has devoted a large portion of the book to vinegar. She regards it as one of the most versatile natural cleaners. Just like her grandmother, she kindly teaches the reader how to use this "cleaning wonder." Of course, Black also recommends that you use many different kinds of natural cleaners.

Anyone interested in cleaning everyday things without hurting the environment should read this informative and entertaining book.

32. Q: According to the passage, what is Your #1 Dry Cleaner's?

(a) A highly successful company specializing in selling natural cleaners
(b) A moderately successful company aimed at protecting the environment
(c) A successful company that Ms. Black acquired when she was very young
(d) A cleaning company operated by the author of the book in question

33. Q: What can be inferred from the review?

(a) Ms. Black has developed her musical talent to the highest degree.
(b) Vinegar is Ms. Black's favorite natural cleaner.
(c) Cleaning Floors was opposed to the publication of the book in question.
(d) Ms. Black is concerned that chemical cleaners will degrade the environment.

Questions 34-35

Dear Mr. and Mrs. Smith:

Thank you for attending the PTA meeting last Thursday. I instantly realized that both of you care deeply about your daughter Erica. As her homeroom teacher, I am doing my best to help her adjust to her new school. I am convinced that she will settle in soon. Everybody loves her, and I hope that she will feel welcomed and loved.

I must mention that Erica is an unusually brilliant student. She excels in almost every subject, except history. She seems to believe that remembering events and dates is what history is all about. However, history helps us understand complex relationships between historic events. Unfortunately, because of time constraints, I cannot make her become interested in understanding such relationships. Therefore, I recommend that she read historical novels written by renowned authors such as William Golding.

If you want to discuss anything about her school life, feel free to email me at laurad@christianhigh.org.

Sincerely yours,

Laura Davis
History Teacher
Christian High School

34. Q: What is the main purpose of the letter?

(a) To appreciate the efforts of Mr. and Mrs. Smith in making PTA meetings more productive
(b) To praise Mr. and Mrs. Smith for helping Erica improve her school life
(c) To thank the recipients for getting a brilliant student to attend her school
(d) To encourage the recipients to help their child to understand history better

35. Q: Which statement would the author most likely agree with?

(a) Erica's exceptional intelligence is an unsurmountable obstacle to making friends.
(b) The Smiths are not fully aware of Erica's enormous potential.
(c) History may help us understand complex relationships between events.
(d) Face-to-face interaction is less effective than e-mail exchanges.

You have reached the end of the Reading Comprehension section. Please remain seated until you are dismissed by the proctor. You are NOT allowed to turn to any other section of the test.

TEPS
Test of English Proficiency
developed by
Seoul National University

앞면(Side1)

청해 Listening Comprehension
(Questions 1–40, answer bubbles a/b/c/d)

어휘 Vocabulary
(Questions 1–30, answer bubbles a/b/c/d)

문법 Grammar
(Questions 1–30, answer bubbles a/b/c/d)

독해 Reading Comprehension
(Questions 1–35, answer bubbles a/b/c/d)

수험번호 Registration No.
성명 Name 한글 / 한자
문제지번호 Test Booklet No.
감독관확인란

주민등록번호 National ID No.
수험번호 Registration No.
비밀번호 Password
좌석번호 Seat No.
고사실번호 Room No.

서 약
본인은 필기구 및 기재오류와 답안지 훼손으로 인한 책임을 지고, 부정행위 처리규정을 준수할 것을 서약합니다.

답안작성시 유의사항

1. 답안 작성은 반드시 **컴퓨터용 싸인펜**을 사용해야 합니다.
2. 답안을 정정할 경우 **수정테이프(수정액 불가)**를 사용해야 합니다.
3. 본 답안지는 컴퓨터로 처리되므로 훼손해서는 안되며, 답안지 하단의 타이밍마크(❙❙)를 찢거나, 낙서 등으로 인한 훼손시 불이익이 발생할 수 있습니다.

4. 답안은 문항당 정답을 1개만 골라 ● 와 같이 정확히 기재하여야 하며, 필기구 오류나 본인의 부주의로 잘못 표기한 경우에는 답 관리위원회의 OMR판독기의 판독결과에 따르며, 그 결과는 본인이 책임집니다.
   Good ● Bad ⊙ ◐ ◯ ⊗ ⊘
5. 감독관의 확인이 없는 답안지는 무효처리됩니다.

TEPS

Test of English Proficiency
developed by
Seoul National University

Answer Keys_TEST 2

Listening Comprehension

1 (b)	2 (c)	3 (b)	4 (c)	5 (d)	6 (a)	7 (b)	8 (c)	9 (b)	10 (d)
11 (c)	12 (b)	13 (a)	14 (c)	15 (d)	16 (c)	17 (c)	18 (a)	19 (d)	20 (b)
21 (c)	22 (b)	23 (a)	24 (d)	25 (d)	26 (c)	27 (c)	28 (b)	29 (d)	30 (b)
31 (a)	32 (a)	33 (d)	34 (b)	35 (c)	36 (c)	37 (d)	38 (b)	39 (c)	40 (b)

Vocabulary

1 (c)	2 (d)	3 (d)	4 (b)	5 (c)	6 (b)	7 (b)	8 (a)	9 (c)	10 (c)
11 (c)	12 (b)	13 (d)	14 (c)	15 (d)	16 (d)	17 (d)	18 (d)	19 (b)	20 (b)
21 (c)	22 (c)	23 (d)	24 (d)	25 (d)	26 (b)	27 (b)	28 (b)	29 (d)	30 (d)

Grammar

1 (c)	2 (b)	3 (b)	4 (c)	5 (a)	6 (a)	7 (a)	8 (a)	9 (d)	10 (c)
11 (b)	12 (c)	13 (b)	14 (b)	15 (a)	16 (c)	17 (b)	18 (b)	19 (b)	20 (d)
21 (b)	22 (b)	23 (b)	24 (a)	25 (a)	26 (b)	27 (c)	28 (b)	29 (d)	30 (d)

Reading Comprehension

1 (b)	2 (a)	3 (b)	4 (c)	5 (c)	6 (b)	7 (c)	8 (d)	9 (c)	10 (c)
11 (b)	12 (b)	13 (b)	14 (c)	15 (d)	16 (c)	17 (c)	18 (d)	19 (c)	20 (c)
21 (b)	22 (d)	23 (c)	24 (b)	25 (b)	26 (b)	27 (c)	28 (b)	29 (b)	30 (c)
31 (d)	32 (d)	33 (d)	34 (d)	35 (c)					

NEW TEPS 실전 모의고사 3회분

지은이 김무룡, 넥서스 TEPS연구소
펴낸이 임상진
펴낸곳 (주)넥서스

출판신고 1992년 4월 3일 제311-2002-2호
10880 경기도 파주시 지목로 5
Tel (02)330-5500 Fax (02)330-5555

ISBN 979-11-6165-317-4 13740

저자와 출판사의 허락 없이 내용의 일부를 인용하거나
발췌하는 것을 금합니다.

가격은 뒤표지에 있습니다.
잘못 만들어진 책은 구입처에서 바꾸어 드립니다.

www.nexusbook.com

NEW TEPS
실전 모의고사

새롭게 바뀐 NEW TEPS를 대비하는 실전 모의고사

★ 서울대텝스관리위원회 NEW TEPS 경향 완벽 반영

★ 실제 NEW TEPS 시험지 그대로 구성한 실전 모의고사 3회분 수록

★ 청해 스크립트 및 쉽고 자세한 해석/해설 온라인 무료 다운로드 제공

★ NEW TEPS 실전용·복습용·고사장 버전의 3종 MP3 무료 다운로드

★ 청취력 향상을 위한 온라인/모바일 받아쓰기 테스트 제공

QR코드 / www.nexusbook.com

MP3를 가장 빠르고 쉽게 듣는 방법

❶ 구글 플레이, 앱스토어에서 "콜롬북스" 어플 설치
❷ 도서명으로 검색
❸ 실전용, 복습용, 고사장 버전 3종 MP3 다운로드

MP3 바로 듣기
해석·해설 확인
받아쓰기 테스트

TEST 3

TEPS

Test of English Proficiency
developed by
Seoul National University

NEW TEPS 시험 구성

영역	문제 유형	문항수	제한 시간	점수 범위
청해 Listening Comprehension	Part I: 한 문장을 듣고 이어질 대화로 가장 적절한 답 고르기 (문장 1회 청취 후 선택지 1회 청취)	10	40분	0~240점
	Part II: 짧은 대화를 듣고 이어질 대화로 가장 적절한 답 고르기 (대화 1회 청취 후 선택지 1회 청취)	10		
	Part III: 긴 대화를 듣고 질문에 가장 적절한 답 고르기 (대화 및 질문 1회 청취 후 선택지 1회 청취)	10		
	Part IV: 담화를 듣고 질문에 가장 적절한 답 고르기(1지문 1문항) (담화 및 질문 2회 청취 후 선택지 1회 청취)	6		
	신유형 Part V: 담화를 듣고 질문에 가장 적절한 답 고르기(1지문 2문항) (담화 및 질문 2회 청취 후 선택지 1회 청취)	4		
어휘 Vocabulary	Part I: 대화문의 빈칸에 가장 적절한 어휘 고르기	10	통합 25분	0~60점
	Part II: 단문의 빈칸에 가장 적절한 어휘 고르기	20		
문법 Grammar	Part I: 대화문의 빈칸에 가장 적절한 답 고르기	10		0~60점
	Part II: 단문의 빈칸에 가장 적절한 답 고르기	15		
	Part III: 대화 및 문단에서 문법상 틀리거나 어색한 부분 고르기	5		
독해 Reading Comprehension	Part I: 지문을 읽고 빈칸에 가장 적절한 답 고르기	10	40분	0~240점
	Part II: 지문을 읽고 문맥상 어색한 내용 고르기	2		
	Part III: 지문을 읽고 질문에 가장 적절한 답 고르기(1지문 1문항)	13		
	신유형 Part IV: 지문을 읽고 질문에 가장 적절한 답 고르기(1지문 2문항)	10		
총계	14개 Parts	135문항	105분	0~600점

TEPS

LISTENING COMPREHENSION

DIRECTIONS

1. In the Listening Comprehension section, all content will be presented orally rather than in written form.
2. This section contains five parts. For each part, you will receive separate instructions. Listen to the instructions carefully, and choose the best answer from the options for each item.

MP3 바로 듣기
해석·해설 확인
받아쓰기 테스트

Part I Questions 1~10

You will now hear ten individual spoken questions or statements, each followed by four spoken responses. Choose the most appropriate response for each item.

Part II Questions 11~20

You will now hear ten short conversation fragments, each followed by four spoken responses. Choose the most appropriate response to complete each conversation.

Part III Questions 21~30

You will now hear ten complete conversations. For each conversation, you will be asked to answer a question. Before each conversation, you will hear a short description of the situation. After listening to the description and conversation once, you will hear a question and four options. Based on the given information, choose the option that best answers the question.

Part IV Questions 31~36

You will now hear six short talks. After each talk, you will be asked to answer a question. Each talk and its corresponding question will be read twice. Then you will hear four options which will be read only once. Based on the given information, choose the option that best answers the question.

Part V **Questions 37~40**

You will now hear two longer talks. After each talk, you will be asked to answer two questions. Each talk and its corresponding questions will be read twice. However, the four options for each question will be read only once. Based on the given information, choose the option that best answers each question.

TEPS

Vocabulary & Grammar

Directions

These two sections test your vocabulary and grammar knowledge. You will have 25 minutes to complete a total of 60 questions: 30 from the Vocabulary section and 30 from the Grammar section. Be sure to follow the directions given by the proctor.

Part I Questions 1~10

Choose the option that best completes each dialogue.

1. A: If the economy doesn't improve we won't be able to pay our debts.
   B: Yeah, it could _____ an end to the business.
   (a) toil
   (b) spell
   (c) infuse
   (d) project

2. A: Did you get much of your assignment done today?
   B: Yes, I made a lot of _____.
   (a) forwards
   (b) progress
   (c) steps
   (d) wins

3. A: Excuse me, where are the job application forms?
   B: There's a _____ of them at the end of the counter.
   (a) peel
   (b) stack
   (c) block
   (d) portion

4. A: Why are you reluctant to come out with us on Saturday?
   B: I'll be _____ on time this weekend.
   (a) tiny
   (b) lack
   (c) short
   (d) empty

5. A: Can you advise me on our schedule tomorrow?
   B: Sure, wait a moment and I'll _____.
   (a) go out on a limb
   (b) walk you through it
   (c) bend over backwards
   (d) drive you up the wall

6. A: Is your father still lacking energy after his heart attack?
   B: I'm afraid so. He's still quite _____.
   (a) belated
   (b) encrusted
   (c) debilitated
   (d) formulated

7. A: Did you get in much trouble with the boss?
   B: I just got a(n) _____. Nothing more.
   (a) blister
   (b) fallacy
   (c) reprimand
   (d) altercation

8. A: Is there any way we can tour the island easily?
   B: The hotel will arrange a(n) _____ for us.
   (a) pack
   (b) appraisal
   (c) excursion
   (d) schematic

9. A: You're certainly hostile to our company president.
   B: I see him as nothing but _____.
   (a) diligent
   (b) delectable
   (c) indigenous
   (d) incompetent

10. A: People in management failed to act in time to save the company.
    B: I agree. It was all due to their _____.
    (a) carefulness
    (b) fortitude
    (c) negligence
    (d) conservation

Part II Questions 11~30

Choose the option that best completes each sentence.

11. Humans, though not affected by foot-and-mouth disease, can pass it on as _____.

    (a) evictors
    (b) carriers
    (c) reflectors
    (d) passengers

12. The reason for the disappearance of the great Indus Valley Civilization is a mystery and still _____ scholars.

    (a) flaws
    (b) defiles
    (c) tarnishes
    (d) confounds

13. Offensive or abusive comments will be removed and offenders may be prevented from further _____.

    (a) submission
    (b) exception
    (c) despondency
    (d) consolation

14. As a government, we are _____ to putting children first and to ensuring a better life for the most vulnerable members of our society.

    (a) supplied
    (b) arrested
    (c) entranced
    (d) committed

15. Learn about the latest property hotspots and get _____ mortgage advice from our team of experts.

    (a) placid
    (b) invaluable
    (c) appetizing
    (d) extraneous

16. It is _____ to suggest that violence on television will cause everyone to act violently because that does not happen.

    (a) tenable
    (b) variable
    (c) implausible
    (d) uncountable

17. William Golding was considered one of the most original and _____ novelists of his time after publishing *Lord of the Flies*.

    (a) replenished
    (b) pernicious
    (c) formidable
    (d) slovenly

18. The hardness of a diamond is due to the strong _____ forces between the carbon atoms of which it is made.

    (a) glutinous
    (b) cohesive
    (c) ornamental
    (d) probationary

19. Despite hard times in Detroit, Stan's Diner continues to _____ with its low prices and quality service.

    (a) forage
    (b) renege
    (c) prosper
    (d) migrate

20. Image-stabilization technologies are used to _____ for and largely overcome the shake and jitter common to digital camcorders and cameras.

    (a) balance
    (b) compensate
    (c) neutralize
    (d) recompense

21. Geoffrey Chaucer's *The Canterbury Tales* reflects a society in _____, when a middle class was emerging out of England's feudal system.

    (a) modality
    (b) transition
    (c) heraldry
    (d) refraction

22. Teachers often feel the _____ of educational budget cuts and have to put up with inadequate facilities and poor pay rates.

    (a) effects
    (b) heaves
    (c) strokes
    (d) remnants

23. According to the UN Environment Program, more than a million seabirds are killed every year because of plastic _____ in the ocean.

    (a) debris
    (b) cartloads
    (c) shingles
    (d) stains

24. Setting standards in the defense industry and pursuing allegations of _____ is the proper course for any national government.

    (a) tenacity
    (b) precaution
    (c) misconduct
    (d) discomfort

25. After a head injury, the man's personality changed dramatically and he went from being _____, polite, and thoughtful to rude, reckless, and socially irresponsible.

    (a) irate
    (b) satiric
    (c) provocative
    (d) conscientious

26. A former Costa Rican President was sentenced to five years in prison Monday for _____ funds intended for public hospitals.

    (a) dredging
    (b) embezzling
    (c) ingesting
    (d) bereaving

27. Although most people live fairly easily in hot environments, they do not _____ well to cold ones.

    (a) transpose
    (b) adapt
    (c) season
    (d) officiate

28. Exercising and _____ in mental tasks such as chess or crossword puzzles can slow mental decline and protect against memory loss.

    (a) abstaining
    (b) engaging
    (c) revealing
    (d) grafting

29. Unfortunately, this book is full of _____ arguments whose bold assertions are not backed by any evidence whatsoever.

    (a) chronic
    (b) taciturn
    (c) ludicrous
    (d) elated

30. Excavations of ancient Pompeian houses show they were _____ furnished with marble floors, wall-paintings, statues, tapestries, and bronze tables.

    (a) dejectedly
    (b) malignantly
    (c) imprudently
    (d) sumptuously

You have finished the Vocabulary questions. Please continue on to the Grammar questions.

Part I Questions 1~10

Choose the option that best completes each dialogue.

1. A: It's important to have equal opportunities in the workplace.
   B: Yes, but equality _____ exist everywhere.
   (a) might
   (b) would
   (c) should
   (d) could

2. A: We were in Italy but didn't get to see Venice.
   B: If I _____ to Italy, I would have made sure to visit it.
   (a) went
   (b) had been
   (c) am going
   (d) had been gone

3. A: Which exercise is the best way for me to lose weight?
   B: Well, _____ each day, you could lose five kilos in a month.
   (a) to swim
   (b) you swim
   (c) swimming
   (d) having swum

4. A: Are you sure you can leave work by 5:00?
   B: Yes, I intend _____ all I need to do by then.
   (a) finish
   (b) for finishing
   (c) will be finishing
   (d) to have finished

5. A: Why are there police helicopters hovering around?
   B: A criminal suspect _____ to be in the area.
   (a) believes
   (b) is believed
   (c) was believing
   (d) could be believed

6. A: Do you think Ralph has already passed his driving test?
   B: No, I'm not sure he _____.
   (a) has
   (b) has that
   (c) has the test
   (d) has it passed

7. A: What was wrong with the delivery?
   B: Only one of the books I ordered _____.
   (a) has been delivered
   (b) was being delivered
   (c) have been delivered
   (d) were being delivered

8. A: You're taking a long time choosing a new secretary.
   B: Well, I need an employee _____ I can trust.
   (a) what
   (b) whom
   (c) of that
   (d) by which

9. A: I doubt this country will improve anytime soon.
   B: _____ a corrupt government, it would.
   (a) It wasn't for
   (b) There wasn't
   (c) Were it not for
   (d) Had not it been

10. A: How are your language lessons going?
    B: Not very good. I _____.
    (a) am difficult to learn languages
    (b) have language difficulty to learn
    (c) have difficulty learning languages
    (d) am language learning that is difficult

Part II Questions 11~25

Choose the option that best completes each sentence.

11. More attention must be paid to the effect of the financial crisis on retirees, many _____ depend on interest income to supplement their Social Security.

    (a) at whichever
    (b) of whom
    (c) by what
    (d) in that

12. The affluent era of high salaries and full employment for law grads is over, as the legal profession lurches _____ its worst slump in decades.

    (a) astride
    (b) through
    (c) ahead of
    (d) in between

13. Unless the richest nations come to _____ of weakened states, their financial crisis will have less hope of recovery.

    (a) rescue
    (b) a rescue
    (c) the rescue
    (d) any rescue

14. The movie's intricate plot was masterful, its cinematography is outstanding, _____ there was something lacking in the performances of the leads.

    (a) and yet
    (b) whereby
    (c) but instead
    (d) provided that

15. As awareness of environmental concerns _____, therapists have seen a rise in household bickering, particularly about food.

    (a) grew
    (b) has grown
    (c) was growing
    (d) has been grown

16. _____ the color of the carrot modified to appear orange rather than its original purple.

    (a) The 1500s was it that
    (b) Not until the 1500s was
    (c) Was it not the 1500s until
    (d) Had it not been until 1500s

17. _____ medical devices and laptops, patients can see doctors without leaving home and have their information logged into electronic records.

    (a) Using
    (b) To use
    (c) They use
    (d) Have to use

18. The welfare project _____ without the generosity and help of all of our many volunteers.

    (a) cannot have succeeded
    (b) need not have succeeded
    (c) would not have succeeded
    (d) should not have succeeded

19. Researchers reported that antidepressant drugs seemed to be effective mainly in people with severe depression, not _____ with milder forms.

    (a) ones
    (b) them
    (c) those
    (d) another

20. In the case of a routine offense, unless the student or school official involved specifically requests that the student's parents _____, they shall not be contacted.

    (a) be notified
    (b) are notified
    (c) were notified
    (d) will be notified

14

21. Despite working long hours six days a week, the shop assistant never had more than _____ left over after paying her bills.

    (a) few money
    (b) small monies
    (c) a few monies
    (d) a little money

22. It was _____ cold day and snowing so heavily that it was decided school would be cancelled.

    (a) a very
    (b) such a
    (c) a much
    (d) by far a

23. Clever boutiques and cozy restaurants are emerging in the Fort Point neighborhood, _____ New England's largest concentration of visual artists.

    (a) of home said to be
    (b) said to be home to
    (c) home it is said to be of
    (d) being said it is home for

24. In 1876, the world's first long-distance telephone call _____ in Paris, Ontario, by Alexander Bell from his father and uncle in Brantford, Ontario.

    (a) received
    (b) was received
    (c) has been received
    (d) had been receiving

25. _____, from the brilliantly subversive screenplay to the vivid cinematography, masterful directing, and perfectly paced editing.

    (a) Aspects of film all are top-notch
    (b) Top-notch the film's aspects were
    (c) All aspects of the film are top-notch
    (d) The film was top-notch every aspect

Part III Questions 26~30

Read each dialogue or passage carefully and identify the option that contains a grammatical error.

26. (a) A: Dr. Wortham's lecture made me confusing, especially the last part.
    (b) B: I was exactly the same. I couldn't grasp what he was getting at.
    (c) A: He mentioned Chapter 7 of our textbook. Were we supposed to have read it?
    (d) B: Yeah, I remember him saying something about that. I bet that was the problem.

27. (a) A: Looks like we're out of milk. Weren't you supposed to buy some yesterday?
    (b) B: I'm sorry, but I didn't have time to do any shopping yesterday. I was so busy.
    (c) A: Don't worry. I'll buy the milk in case I go to the supermarket this morning.
    (d) B: Thanks. Actually, I've got some spare time so I'll come and give you a hand.

28. (a) Though it was unique to the clans in northern Australia originally, the didgeridoo is now the most recognizable instrument in Aboriginal music. (b) The classic didgeridoo is made of a termite-hollowed bamboo or eucalyptus tree, as today it's common to find didgeridoos made of plastic pipe. (c) The player of a didgeridoo uses a special breathing technique to blow through the didgeridoo continuously. (d) The sound produced is a low-frequency sound that can be sustained and heard over long distances.

29. (a) For safety and for defense, people in the Middle Ages formed small communities around a central lord or master. (b) Most people lived on a manor, which consisted of the castle, the church, the village, and the surrounding farmland. (c) In this feudal system, the king awarded in return land grants to important nobles for their contribution of soldiers for the king's armies. (d) At the lowest echelon of society were the peasants, who lived and worked on a noble's land and under his protection.

30. (a) Charles Dickens is the well-known author of such classics as *Great Expectations*, *A Christmas Carol*, and *The Adventures of Oliver Twist*. (b) But not many people know that Dickens should be ashamed of his impoverished boyhood and his father's imprisonment. (c) Not even his closest friends or in-laws knew his personal history because he kept it secret. (d) Meanwhile, he consistently championed the rights of the poor and the downtrodden in his writing.

You have reached the end of the Vocabulary & Grammar sections. Do NOT move on to the Reading Comprehension section until instructed to do so. You are NOT allowed to turn to any other section of the test.

TEPS

Reading Comprehension

Directions

This section tests your ability to comprehend reading passages. You will have 40 minutes to complete 35 questions. Be sure to follow the directions given by the proctor.

Part I Questions 1~10

Read the passage and choose the option that best completes the passage.

1. European companies may not be as nimble as their counterparts in the United States, but they are preserving jobs through the global downturn. In the more flexible American labor market, companies responded to the recession by letting workers go, sharply cutting costs and preserving profit margins. European companies, however, reduced hours on the job and made a decision to accept lower profit margins in the short term. They made old plants more modern and effective rather than watching workers or companies deemed uncompetitive fall by the wayside. For the short term at least, they have _____. Nonetheless, they are surviving.

   (a) let workers go and wound down production
   (b) managed to outdo their American competitors
   (c) paid the price in lower profits and productivity
   (d) reduced infrastructure spending to stay in business

2. Immunization is not 100% effective and may result in unpleasant consequences for a very small number of individuals. However, agreement to immunize as a society is a recognition that overall it reduces the incidence of infection and in fact protects those whose immunizations do not work. Health professionals should all be immunized. Those who refuse to do so, especially as they are in contact with many vulnerable people during the day, are refusing to be part of the social contract. It is a very selfish, shortsighted position. I see no reason why they _____.

   (a) were not immunized when they requested it
   (b) should not be reprimanded for refusing to participate
   (c) would ask anyone to sign an unethical contract
   (d) have to immunize those people on a yearly basis

3. Dear Editor,

   This letter is in response to the recent article in your publication disparaging bicycle riders' use of roadways. Impatient drivers have complained of bicycle riders' slowing traffic, but the problem is really with our public street systems. Proposing prohibitions on recreational bicycle travel is not the answer. Some people need to use bicycles because they cannot afford a car or they want to be more environmentally friendly. Others like to ride them to work. These people are entitled to road use as anyone else. So I think the answer is _____.

   Sincerely,
   Jan Stevenson, Cyclist

   (a) for people to use bicycles more often
   (b) to enforce stricter road rules on motorists
   (c) more efficient roadways for mixed traffic
   (d) to lift the restrictions being imposed on us

4. New research has uncovered how plants _____. Plants are incredibly temperature sensitive and can perceive changes of as little as one degree Celsius. However, it has just been discovered that they not only "feel" the temperature rise, but can also coordinate an appropriate response—activating hundreds of genes and deactivating others. These findings may help to explain how plants will respond in the face of climate change. They may prove to be critical for the breeding of more temperature-resistant crops as the world heats up.

   (a) will be the salvation of the planet in the future
   (b) under climate change suffer from genetic mutations
   (c) respond to temperature fluctuations at a genetic level
   (d) can naturally withstand high temperatures over generations

5. Most pet owners know how to tell if their dog is happy and healthy. He will have a shiny, even coat, be eager to play, and have regular eating habits. Signs of a sick dog are not always so easy to spot because dogs have a natural instinct to hide sickness or pain. But as a caring owner, it is your responsibility to know the signs. Refusing to eat is a common warning sign. Vomiting is another, which can indicate a variety of problems. These are not the only signs. Therefore, learn _____.

   (a) what alleviates more severe pain symptoms
   (b) what to watch for and when to go see a vet
   (c) how to tell when your dog is healthy
   (d) how your pet came to behave in that way

6. Ronald Pander's science fiction novel *Scarred Earth* is an unforgettable dark vision of the future. Its setting is a post-apocalyptic world where freedom is restricted by a perverse form of religion and by petty governments. Its narrator, Davy, describes his life in this world, taking us on a journey of self-discovery and questioning. As such, the emphasis in Pander's *Scarred Earth* is on human behavior, morality, and social responsibility, rather than on science, technological gadgets, or apocalyptic survival. This gives the novel a timeless quality. It forces us to ponder _____.

(a) the relevance of religion in our modern world
(b) the reason for Davy's rebellion against society
(c) the nature of human cultures and their societies
(d) the way in which we use science and technology

7. TopClassJobs.com is the first niche recruiting channel to bring together recent PhDs, professors, research institutions, and other employers to find the best match. Our vision is to be the premier source for employers to hire postdocs, research associates, and scientists. Over 100,000 people visit our Web site seeking postdoctoral opportunities each month. Jobs posted on our Web site are normally viewed up to 5,000 times. We have thousands of universities, companies, research institutions, and government agencies worldwide that use our service. Our site is all they need _____.

(a) to attract students eager to pursue a science education
(b) for finding the best employer for their professional talents
(c) to match their desires with the best educational institutional
(d) for the right postgrads and professionals to fill their positions

8. At Dartmouth University, researchers looking into why people have ambition are using brain imaging to investigate the ability to stay focused on a task until it's completed as well as possible. However, the researchers could not determine whether innate differences in the brain were driving ambitious behavior or whether learned behavior was causing it. Some believe it can be learned or sparked into action if the right jolt comes along. They proposed that it might be genetic for some but not necessarily for others. In other words, people can develop a drive to succeed if they _____.

(a) have the genetic predisposition to do so
(b) find the right thing to be ambitious about
(c) show these differences in their brain images
(d) encounter role models who are ambitious

9. I'm one of the many people in the UK now facing unemployment after graduating. They already have a nickname for people like me—the lost generation. We are 1 million 16- to 24-year-olds who are looking for work. Not only that, but we have a huge debt after paying for our education. People like me are feeling incredibly angry, with debts in excess of £20,000. We were told we would get a job at the end of our degrees and earn more money. _____, we're just heavily indebted. What are we all going to do? The future looks very bleak.

(a) Instead
(b) Likewise
(c) Especially
(d) Consequently

10. Being a famous artist in your own lifetime is no guarantee that you'll be remembered by other artists. Have you heard of the French painter Ernest Meissonier? He was a contemporary with Edouard Manet, and by far the more successful artist in terms of critical acclaim and sales. _____, Vincent van Gogh is probably the most famous example of when the reverse is true. Van Gogh relied on his brother, Theo, to provide him with paint and canvas, yet today his paintings fetch record prices whenever they come up at art auctions, and he's a household name.

(a) And yet
(b) In contrast
(c) Despite this
(d) In the same way

Part II Questions 11~12

Read the passage and identify the option that does NOT belong.

11. Peanuts have long been regarded as a very nutritious health food. (a) They were first grown in prehistoric times in South America and were later spread worldwide by European traders. (b) Of all the kinds of nuts, they contain the highest quality of plant protein, making them ideal for children and vegetarians. (c) While they are considered high in fat, they primarily contain good fats, also known as unsaturated fats. (d) In fact, their healthy heart benefits were officially recognized by the U.S. Food and Drug Administration.

12. The Russian finance minister on Wednesday announced a new approach to catching up with the West in technology. (a) Russia's government will order ministries and state companies to buy products that qualify as "innovative" and that are made in Russia. (b) Government support will be extended to everybody who wants to work in this sphere and who wants to work for the future. (c) Translating Russia's bounty of scientific talent into popular products is a problem that has vexed the country since Soviet times. (d) One government effort already in place, in the hope of leapfrogging the West's lead in semiconductors, is funding for nanotechnology.

Part III Questions 13~25

Read the passage, question, and options. Then, based on the given information, choose the option that best answers each question.

13. Are IT applications your specialty? We at Dynaquest need a Computer Director for our IT Business Support Group, San Francisco. You will plan, direct, and coordinate the IT applications development for a multinational company engaged in duty free and luxury merchandise retail for the international traveling public. This position requires highly collaborative skills and teamwork. A minimum of ten years' experience is expected. Send your résumés to IT Support Group at the following email address: personnel@dynaquest.com.

    Q: What is the position being advertised mainly responsible for?
    (a) Directing computer operations for an IT support business
    (b) Developing applications for the international travel industry
    (c) Overseeing development of IT applications for a retail company
    (d) Managing support of IT applications for a global retail company

14.

    To Alex Browne, CEO:

    After an explosion at your Texas refinery in March killed 15 people and injured 170 others, and after two minor explosions last summer, I'm dismayed at the lack of initiative applied to solving the root causes. Your underlying management philosophy has failed in a true marriage of words and deeds. You said all the right things about a commitment to safety, yet correspondences I have unearthed show intentions to the contrary. Too much of what you've done smacks of public relations countermeasures. Can you inform me how you can continue to operate despite serious safety risks known to your company? I await your response.

    Sincerely yours,

    Wayne Baxter
    State Independent Safety Committee

    Q: What is mainly discussed about Alex Browne?
    (a) His record of failed safety initiatives as CEO.
    (b) His ongoing hypocritical actions on company safety.
    (c) His managerial finesse in the wake of tragic accidents.
    (d) His commendable commitment to improving worker safety.

15. Most herbal experts agree that ginkgo extract taken from the nuts of a ginkgo tree is useful for modestly improving the mental function of people with mild senile dementia or Alzheimer's disease. Further research, however, has also revealed that ginkgo is more useful than initially thought. An English study showed it may have a much broader memory-boosting ability, when it found improved short-term memory and reaction time across all ages after people were given a single 120mg dose of ginkgo. The one-time dose worked in older people best, but also improved concentration, focus, and alertness for younger people.

Q: What is the main idea of the passage?
(a) Ginkgo can assist people who have mental problems.
(b) Ginkgo is the best way to increase your mental powers.
(c) Gingko improves mental capabilities across all age groups.
(d) Ginkgo is recommended for older rather than younger people.

16. Robert Hilton made a name for himself with spy thrillers set during the Cold War and in the Middle East. In his latest novel, *Man in the Dark*, corporate greed is the new target of his ire. Though there is a change of direction, it is delivered with the same intellect and penetrating insights we have come to expect from Hilton. The novel leads us into familiar territory, where intrigues of moral uncertainty and paradox hold sway and evil is done in the name of good. With that nihilistic cynicism we find lurking behind his spy novels, Hilton once again unswervingly tackles the key issues of our times.

Q: What is the main idea about Hilton's latest novel?
(a) It bears the hallmarks of his earlier thrillers.
(b) It represents a major literary change for Hilton.
(c) It primarily concentrates on today's moral issues.
(d) It has topics not unlike the ones in his spy novels.

17.

News Report

The Macon County Airport runway extension has been a source of controversy since native artifacts were found on the proposed extension site, and some area residents have voiced concern over their historical and cultural significance. A recent meeting by the Macon County Airport Authority last Tuesday was convened and seven visitors from the public attended. However, the authority did not allow for a public question-and-answer period. Instead, visitors were told their questions would be answered at a later time. Statements made by the visitors ranged from strong criticism to enthusiastic support, which illustrated a sharp community divide over the airport extension.

Q: Which of the following is correct according to the news report?
(a) A Macon County Airport extension has ruined native artifacts.
(b) A recent meeting involved seven Airport Authority members.
(c) The answers to visitor questions were deferred until later.
(d) The airport extension has met with universal disapproval.

18. The Vikings' swift wooden long ships, equipped with both sails and oars, enabled them to mount piratical raids on the coastal monasteries and settlements of the British Isles, Western Europe, and beyond. An average speed of 10 knots could have been achieved and crews of 25 to 60 men would have been common, seated on benches on open decks, although the largest ships could have carried as many 100 or more. Raids in single ships were quite frequent and, before around 850 AD, fleets rarely had more than 100 ships. Much larger fleets of 200 and upwards were recorded later.

Q: Which of the following is correct according to the passage?
(a) Vikings established settlements beyond Western Europe.
(b) Viking long ships never had room for more than 60 men.
(c) Vikings rarely partook in raids with one ship alone.
(d) Viking fleets once comprised 100 ships or less.

19. China has unearthed the fossil of a two-legged carnivorous dinosaur that lived 160 million years ago and which researchers have identified as the earliest known member of a long lineage that includes birds. The fossil had a long, narrow skull, many small teeth, and powerful biceps and forelimbs, which enabled it to hunt lizards, mammals, and reptiles. It is believed the animal was a young adult when it died and was found in orange mudstone beds in China's western region. The dinosaur has some unique features but it shares some features with birds, such as its head, vertebral column, and hindlimbs.

Q: Which of the following is correct according to the passage?
(a) A fossil found in China was of a dinosaur that ate meat.
(b) China's dinosaur fossil was uncovered with fossils of birds.
(c) A Chinese fossil showed that it had a long, narrow set of teeth.
(d) China's recently discovered dinosaur had descended from a bird.

20. Exercise physiologists agree that if your sport is affected by gravity, such as running, you are penalized for excess weight. So, what is the ideal weight for your sport? For runners, as a general rule, a 1 percent reduction in weight leads to a 1 percent increase in performance. However, everyone has a point at which further weight loss actually makes performance worse. The problem is people vary so there is no formula for the perfect weight, which is where you can stop your body burning its own muscle protein for fuel. It is a matter of trial and error.

Q: Which of the following is correct according to the passage?
(a) Runners with thinner legs achieve better speed.
(b) Ideally, runners should maintain 10 percent body fat.
(c) Running performance varies according to muscle tone.
(d) Each runner has to gauge ideal weight by experimenting.

21.

> ### Pedal across Boston!
>
> Boston Bikers is pleased to announce that the 5th Bike Race is set to begin on May 18th.
>
> - The entrance fee is $100. A first aid kit, drinking water, and snacks as well as a lunch box are included in the fee.
> - Participants must submit their entrance fees by May 1st.
> - Prizes and medals will be given to the first five arriving participants. Other participants will also receive medals.
>
> 10% of the entrance fee will be donated to the Boston Red Cross, so join a refreshing bike ride for a good cause.

Q: Which of the following is correct about the 5th Bike Race?
(a) It is free for all participants.
(b) All of the participants will receive medals.
(c) All of its profits go to the Boston Red Cross.
(d) Children are not allowed to enroll.

22. Among the sand dunes of the Sands of Samar in Israel, a new and previously unknown species of spider has been discovered by a team of scientists. The spider's leg-span can reach up to 14 centimeters, which makes it the largest spider of its type in the Middle East. Although the spider has only just been discovered, it is known that it is a nocturnal spider, mostly active in the hottest months of the year. It has also been discovered that it constructs an underground den which is closed with a "trapdoor" made of sand particles that are glued together to camouflage the den.

Q: Which of the following is correct about the spider according to the passage?
(a) It is known to reach up to 14 centimeters long.
(b) It is the largest spider found in the Mediterranean.
(c) It is primarily active at night rather than during the day.
(d) It is found living in webs that are well camouflaged.

23. My three-hour drive from the city deep into a great Canadian forest for a weekend escape was once a weekend ritual. I wanted to get back to nature, but I would eventually regard this as an ordeal. It was a long, rough drive on gravel tracks to my tiny forest dwelling, a cheap weatherboard shack with no heating. It wasn't even near a lake. I'd get there late at night and be greeted by insects incessantly biting at me. The next day I'd spend a lot of time cleaning the shack. Before long, I realized there's only so much nature one can handle.

Q: What can be inferred about the writer of the passage?
(a) He built his shack by himself over many weekends.
(b) He held respect for those who live among nature.
(c) He eventually lost enthusiasm for weekend getaways.
(d) He prefers living in the country to living in the city.

24. Technology companies are now branching out into the pet business and designing pet products for busy pet owners. One example is the Play Ball. It plays recorded messages from the owner and dispenses treats at random when it's rolled around, so owners can be less worried about their pet feeling alone or bored. Pet Music is a CD that plays soothing music customized to the hearing sensitivities of dogs or cats. It can soothe lonely pets. Lastly, the LaserCat sends a laser dot across the floor to keep your cat entertained when you are away.

Q: What can be inferred from the passage?
(a) Pets that are ignored can become unhealthy.
(b) Some pet owners use technology to alleviate guilt.
(c) Technology has ironically made people's lives busier.
(d) Economic wealth has increased spending on technology.

25.

Jackson Shopping Center

Starting this month October until the end of December, special 20% discount coupons issued by Jackson Shopping Center each month may apply to any products! All furniture is available including

- Dining tables for sharing meals and being together
- Comfortable chairs for spending time concentrating on the job in hand
- Stylish sofas and couches for comfort
- Perfect beds for beauty sleep
- Wardrobes with a variety of styles and sizes

We're offering free delivery on all furniture purchased this month.

Business Hours
Monday – Saturday: 10 A.M. – 6 P.M.
Sunday: 11 A.M. – 5 P.M.

Q: What can be inferred about Jackson Shopping Center from the advertisement?
(a) It sells only office furniture.
(b) Its hours of operation have changed recently.
(c) It will be open until 5 P.M. next month.
(d) The sale offer does not include free delivery on December.

Part IV Questions 26~35

Read the passage, question, and options. Then, based on the given information, choose the option that best answers each question.

Questions 26-27

Audition for a Different Ophelia

Have you ever dreamed of performing on stage? Dreamed of making people laugh and cry by your acting abilities? Dreamed of touching people's hearts and souls? Then, come to William Shakespeare Theatre to audition for Ophelia at 3:00 p.m. on May 15th, 2018!

You might wonder why we are holding an audition for this tragic character from *Hamlet*. Well, we reinterpret her role completely and want our audiences to "see old things in new ways." We interpret Ophelia's madness as her desperate attempt to reclaim her independence. In other words, we believe that in her burning desire to be free again, she goes insane.

On the audition day, you will be given a script to read from. When reading it, keep in mind that the Ophelia you will play is completely different from the Ophelia you are familiar with. Should you have any questions, email Jennifer Hamilton at Jennifer@william-shakespeare.com.

26. Q: Which of the following is correct according to the announcement?

   (a) The theater accepts video submissions from candidates.
   (b) On May 15th, 2018, the theater offers auditions for all characters from *Hamlet*.
   (c) The theater breaks away from the traditional interpretation of Ophelia.
   (d) Audition candidates can either improvise or prepare their own scripts.

27. Q: What can be inferred from the announcement?

   (a) The theater specializes in performances based on religious plays.
   (b) The theater understands that Ophelia is a highly ludicrous character.
   (c) Ms. Hamilton has suggested that the play *Hamlet* be interpreted differently.
   (d) Some audition candidates might find it challenging to play Ophelia.

Questions 28-29

Dear Dr. Benford:

Thank you for your interest in publishing your paper in our journal. As you already know, we specialize in publishing scientifically sound and peer-reviewed research articles. We firmly believe that scientific research should be based on observation and experimentation. At the same time, it is our bone-deep belief that all research papers should be reviewed by fellow scientists.

We regret to inform you that your research paper titled "On the Possibility of the Existence of the Afterlife" has failed to meet our requirements. The so-called afterlife is not a scientifically sound concept in that it is not an object of observation or experimentation. Furthermore, your paper has never been reviewed by any reputable scientists.

You are kindly advised to review and meet our requirements when you try to publish another research paper in our journal.

Sincerely,

Susan Lawrence,
Editor-in-Chief
Empirical Science Journal

28. Q: According to the letter, why has Dr. Benford's paper been rejected?

   (a) Because he has previously submitted the same paper to the journal.
   (b) Because his paper depends heavily on empirical methods.
   (c) Because he is not widely recognized as a reputable scientist.
   (d) Because it has failed to fulfill the criteria for acceptable research papers.

29. Q: What can be inferred from the letter?

   (a) Dr. Benford is highly likely to submit another research paper to the journal.
   (b) The journal is adamant that scientific research methods should be highly valued.
   (c) Observation and experimentation are the most powerful tools for discovering the truth about paranormal phenomena.
   (d) The concept of afterlife is a clearly defined one in the religious community.

Questions 30-31

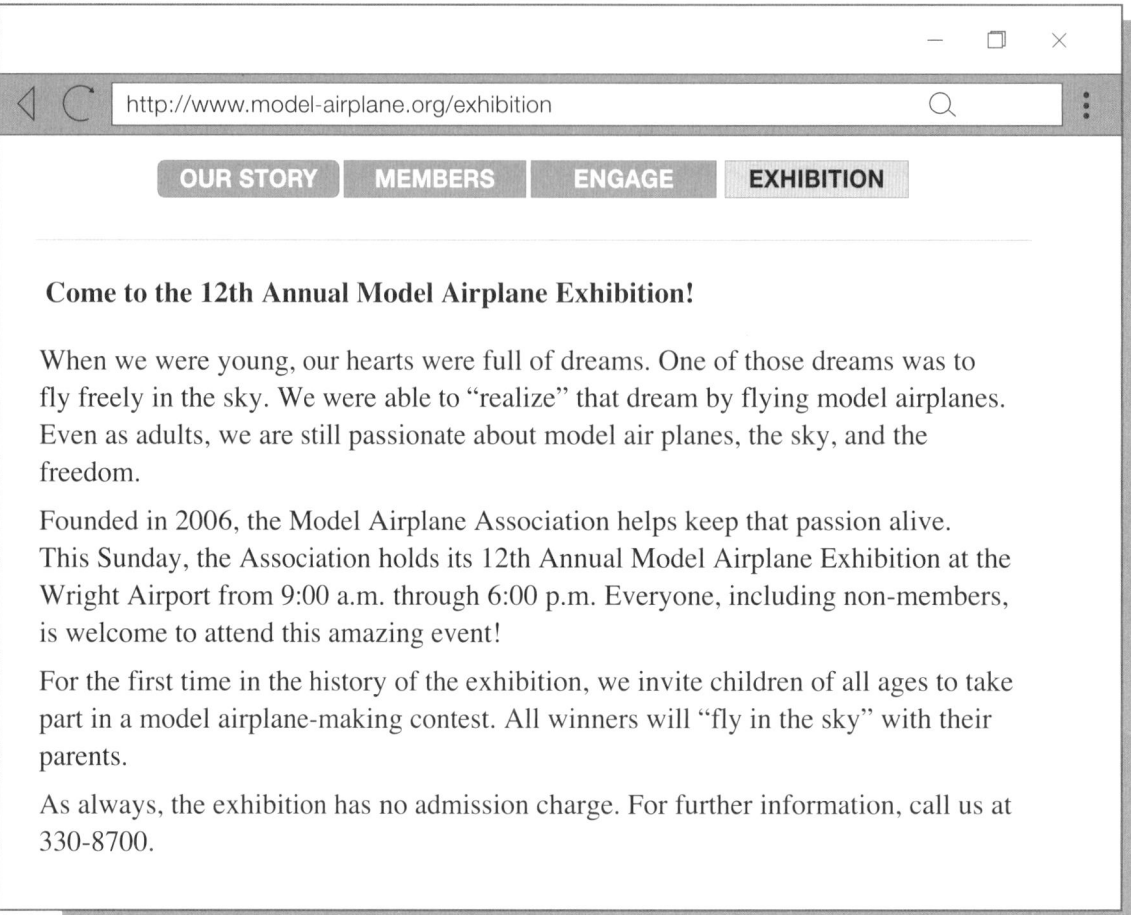

Come to the 12th Annual Model Airplane Exhibition!

When we were young, our hearts were full of dreams. One of those dreams was to fly freely in the sky. We were able to "realize" that dream by flying model airplanes. Even as adults, we are still passionate about model air planes, the sky, and the freedom.

Founded in 2006, the Model Airplane Association helps keep that passion alive. This Sunday, the Association holds its 12th Annual Model Airplane Exhibition at the Wright Airport from 9:00 a.m. through 6:00 p.m. Everyone, including non-members, is welcome to attend this amazing event!

For the first time in the history of the exhibition, we invite children of all ages to take part in a model airplane-making contest. All winners will "fly in the sky" with their parents.

As always, the exhibition has no admission charge. For further information, call us at 330-8700.

30. Q: Which is correct according to the announcement?

  (a) A large number of children have participated in the previous exhibitions.
  (b) Children can compete in the model airplane-making contest in the presence of their legal guardians.
  (c) Additional information on the exhibition can be found at other web pages.
  (d) Members of the association are likely to fly model air planes.

31. Q: What can be inferred from the announcement?

  (a) The association was established to produce highly skilled pilots.
  (b) Children of all ages can become members of the association.
  (c) The Wright Airport has been working with the association for 12 years.
  (d) Some children of the contest will have a chance to take a plane.

Questions 32-33

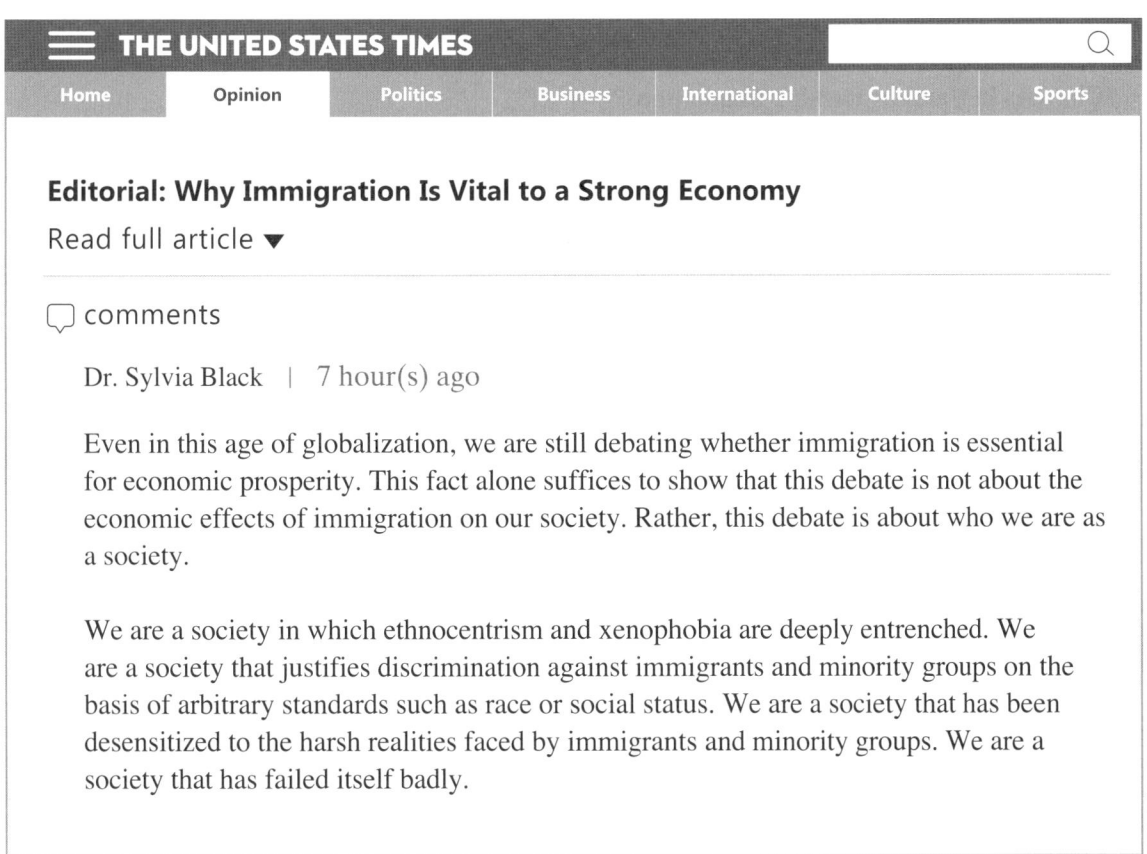

32. Q: What is the main purpose of Dr. Black's comment?

   (a) To criticize American society for failing all its members
   (b) To insist that ethnocentrism is at the root of all social ills
   (c) To clarify the nature of the debate over immigration
   (d) To argue that economic growth is dependent upon immigration

33. Q: Which statement would the author most likely agree with?

   (a) Immigration does not necessarily lead to economic prosperity.
   (b) The economic impacts of immigration on society have been vastly overrated.
   (c) The economic prosperity of American society is hampered by globalization.
   (d) Immigrants and minority groups tend to get a raw deal from society.

Questions 34-35

Changes in Campus Parking Regulations

As you may already know, there have recently been many complaints from visitors about our parking regulations. They say that parking is prohibited in too many locations.

On the one hand, we are aware that we are part of a larger community. On the other hand, the safety of our students and faculty/staff is of paramount importance.

With that in mind, we have decided to introduce the following changes to our parking regulations:

· Visitors can now park in the north and south parking lots.

· Visitors can now apply for Keller-only permits, which require parking in the Keller Parking Lot only.

· Visitors who are graduates of the college are now eligible for free parking.

· Visitors whose family members are students at the college are now eligible to receive a 50% discount on parking permits.

· Visitors whose family members are staff members at the college are now eligible to receive a 60% discount on parking permits.

· Visitors whose family members are on the faculty at the college are now eligible to receive a 70% discount on parking permits.

34. Q: Which of the following visitors will receive the most discount on parking permits?

   (a) Jenny, who knows a graduate of the college
   (b) Amy, whose mother is a professor at the college
   (c) Tom, whose sister is a student at the college
   (d) John, who applies for a Keller-only permit

35. Q: What can be inferred from the notice?

   (a) The college has been notorious for adopting hostile attitudes toward outsiders.
   (b) The college stresses the importance of protecting academic integrity.
   (c) The college's decisions about parking regulations can be swayed by visitors.
   (d) Many visitors complained that parking permits were exorbitantly expensive.

You have reached the end of the Reading Comprehension section. Please remain seated until you are dismissed by the proctor. You are NOT allowed to turn to any other section of the test.

TEPS
Test of English Proficiency developed by Seoul National University

TPS
Test of English Proficiency
developed by
Seoul National University

응시일자 : 20   년   월   일

〈부정행위 및 규정위반 처리규정〉

1. 모든 부정행위 및 규정위반 적발 및 이에 대한 조치는 TEPS관리위원회의 처리규정에 따라 이루어집니다.

2. 부정행위 및 규정위반 행위는 현장 적발 뿐만 아니라 사후에도 적발될 수 있으며 모두 동일한 조치가 취해집니다.

3. 부정행위 적발 시 당해 성적은 무효 처리되며 사안에 따라 최대 5년까지 TEPS관리위원회에서 주관하는 모든 시험의 응시자격이 제한됩니다.

4. 문제지 이외에 메모를 하는 행위와 시험 문제의 일부 또는 전부를 유출하거나 공개하는 경우 부정행위로 처리됩니다.

5. 각 파트별 시간을 준수하지 않거나, 시험 종료 후 답안 작성을 계속할 경우 규정위반으로 처리됩니다.

단체구분

학생 ○   일반 ○

질문란

1. 귀하의 TEPS 응시목적은?
   a) 입사지원 b) 인사정책
   c) 개인실력측정 d) 입시
   e) 국가고시지원 f) 기타

2. 귀하의 영어권 체류 경험은?
   a) 없다 b) 6개월 미만
   c) 6개월이상 1년 미만 d) 1년 이상 3년 미만
   e) 3년 이상 5년 미만 f) 5년 이상

3. 귀하께서 응시하고 계신 고사장에 대한 만족도는?
   a) 0점 b) 1점
   c) 2점 d) 3점
   e) 4점 f) 5점

4. 최근 2년내 TEPS 응시횟수는?
   a) 없다 b) 1회
   c) 2회 d) 3회
   e) 4회 f) 5회 이상

성 명 (성·이름순으로 기재)

성: HONG GIL
명: DONG

성명 영문 ___
   서명 ___

학력

학력	졸업	재학/휴학
초등학교	○	○
중학교	○	○
고등학교	○	○
전문대학	○	○
대학교	○	○
대학원	○	○

전공

인문학 · 어학계열
사회과학 · 법학계열
경제학 · 경영학계열
자연 · 이학계열
의학 · 약학 · 간호학계열
공학계열
예 · 체능계열
음악 · 미술 · 체육계열
기타

직업

공무원
고시준비
교사
군인
의료인
자영업
학생
회사원
무직
기타

직종

임원
환경
자금
공무
생산관리
품질관리
연구
정보/전산관리
생산
서비스
기타

직책

회장
부장
차장
과장
대리
계장
사원
인턴
기타

직위

고위직
전문직(과학/공학)
전문직(교육)
전문직(법률/회계/금융)
기술직
경영
행정
영업
총무
인사
경리
연구

Answer Keys_TEST 3

Listening Comprehension

1 (c)	2 (d)	3 (d)	4 (a)	5 (b)	6 (b)	7 (d)	8 (b)	9 (a)	10 (d)
11 (c)	12 (d)	13 (b)	14 (a)	15 (a)	16 (c)	17 (d)	18 (b)	19 (b)	20 (d)
21 (b)	22 (d)	23 (a)	24 (d)	25 (c)	26 (c)	27 (a)	28 (a)	29 (b)	30 (c)
31 (a)	32 (c)	33 (b)	34 (b)	35 (d)	36 (b)	37 (d)	38 (a)	39 (d)	40 (b)

Vocabulary

1 (b)	2 (b)	3 (b)	4 (c)	5 (b)	6 (c)	7 (c)	8 (c)	9 (d)	10 (c)
11 (b)	12 (d)	13 (a)	14 (d)	15 (b)	16 (c)	17 (c)	18 (b)	19 (c)	20 (b)
21 (b)	22 (a)	23 (a)	24 (c)	25 (d)	26 (b)	27 (b)	28 (b)	29 (c)	30 (d)

Grammar

1 (c)	2 (b)	3 (c)	4 (d)	5 (b)	6 (a)	7 (a)	8 (b)	9 (c)	10 (c)
11 (b)	12 (b)	13 (c)	14 (a)	15 (b)	16 (b)	17 (a)	18 (c)	19 (c)	20 (a)
21 (d)	22 (b)	23 (b)	24 (b)	25 (c)	26 (a)	27 (c)	28 (b)	29 (c)	30 (b)

Reading Comprehension

1 (c)	2 (b)	3 (c)	4 (c)	5 (b)	6 (c)	7 (d)	8 (b)	9 (a)	10 (b)
11 (a)	12 (c)	13 (c)	14 (b)	15 (c)	16 (a)	17 (c)	18 (d)	19 (a)	20 (d)
21 (b)	22 (c)	23 (c)	24 (b)	25 (d)	26 (c)	27 (d)	28 (d)	29 (b)	30 (d)
31 (d)	32 (c)	33 (d)	34 (b)	35 (c)					

독점 출간

가장 최신 텝스 기출 문제를 수록한
서울대 텝스 관리위원회
텝스 최신기출 1200제 시리즈

서울대 텝스 관리위원회
텝스 최신기출 1200제
문제집/해설집 1

서울대 텝스 관리위원회
텝스 최신기출 1200제
문제집/해설집 2

서울대 텝스 관리위원회
텝스 최신기출 1200제
문제집/해설집 3

서울대 텝스 관리위원회 최신 기출 문제는 넥서스에서 독점 출간합니다.

NEW TEPS 실전 모의고사 3회분

지은이 김무룡, 넥서스 TEPS연구소
펴낸이 임상진
펴낸곳 (주)넥서스

출판신고 1992년 4월 3일 제311-2002-2호
10880 경기도 파주시 지목로 5
Tel (02)330-5500 Fax (02)330-5555
ISBN 979-11-6165-317-4 13740

저자와 출판사의 허락 없이 내용의 일부를 인용하거나
발췌하는 것을 금합니다.

가격은 뒤표지에 있습니다.
잘못 만들어진 책은 구입처에서 바꾸어 드립니다.

www.nexusbook.com

NEW TEPS
실전 모의고사

새롭게 바뀐 NEW TEPS를 대비하는 실전 모의고사

★ 서울대텝스관리위원회 NEW TEPS 경향 완벽 반영

★ 실제 NEW TEPS 시험지 그대로 구성한 실전 모의고사 3회분 수록

★ 청해 스크립트 및 쉽고 자세한 해석/해설 온라인 무료 다운로드 제공

★ NEW TEPS 실전용·복습용·고사장 버전의 3종 MP3 무료 다운로드

★ 청취력 향상을 위한 온라인/모바일 받아쓰기 테스트 제공

QR코드 / www.nexusbook.com

MP3를 가장 빠르고 쉽게 듣는 방법

❶ 구글 플레이, 앱스토어에서 "콜롬북스" 어플 설치
❷ 도서명으로 검색
❸ 실전용, 복습용, 고사장 버전 3종 MP3 다운로드

MP3 바로 듣기
해석·해설 확인
받아쓰기 테스트